A
SURVEY
OF
MODERN
GRAMMARS

A
SURVEY
OF
MODERN
GRAMMARS

JEANNE H. HERNDON
Dominican College of San Rafael

HOLT, RINEHART AND WINSTON, INC.
New York · Chicago · San Francisco · Atlanta
Dallas · Montreal · Toronto · London · Sydney

PREFACE

This handbook is intended for those who would like to know something of the findings of linguistic scholarship—especially with regard to the workings of the grammar of the English language—without necessarily wishing to become accomplished linguists themselves. The primary audience is presumed to be in-service and preservice elementary and secondary teachers of the language arts or English, but it is my sincere belief that any intelligent speaker of English will find added insight into the workings of his language in these pages.

I have written as simply as it is possible for me to write and have used very little of the enormously fascinating, but frustratingly complex, detail of scholarly introductions to linguistic investigation and theory. Whenever linguistic terminology has been used, a careful attempt has been made to define terms and explain concepts as clearly as possible. A great many terms to be found in linguistics texts have been eliminated here because it was felt that they could be safely omitted without serious detriment to an overall grasp of the principles involved. Those unfamiliar terms that remain are not pure linguistic lingo. They are terms coined for new concepts in language study, and they have no counterparts in traditional terminology.

The field of language study, like most other areas of intellectual inquiry, has seen a virtual information explosion over the past several decades. Some of this information represents profoundly intelligent and important investigation into the communicative skills of man; some of it is pure hogwash. School boards, administrators, and faculties are inundated with "new English" textbooks and teaching materials, most of which claim to be based on linguistics. Many are well-planned, well-written, and quite effective in the hands of competent teachers; others have little to recommend them beyond the word *linguistic* in their sales brochures.

No effort is made here to judge between the worthwhile and the spurious. It seemed more realistic to attempt to place enough information in the hands of intelligent teachers, parents, and school administrators to give them some basis for making their own judgments. My primary goal has been to give teachers some of the background necessary for them to use the best of the new materials as effectively as possible, for it is my absolutely unshakable conviction that the fundamental processes in education are still firmly in the hands of teachers. Modern, well-equipped buildings, well-written, colorfully illustrated texts, elaborate audiovisual equipment, and complex teaching machines can help competent, dedicated teachers enormously; these things will never replace teachers.

This handbook began as a series of study guides for those in-service and preservice teachers who were students in my Modern Grammars classes. The students were expected to make use of the more complete works available on the history of the language and linguistic study —traditional, structural, and transformational-generative grammar. These works, primarily written for beginning students in linguistics, or made up of articles reprinted from linguistics journals, often assumed a knowledge of terminology and method that most students simply did not have. Those who were approaching this material for the first time were unable to see the beauties of the linguistic forest because they were surrounded by towering trees of unfamiliar detail. The attempt here has been to provide a mile-high view of the terrain; as a result, much of the detail is lost. The Suggested Reading included at the end of the book might, therefore, better be called Strongly Urged Reading. All should be a part of every English Department faculty library. In choosing these readings, I have made an attempt to list those works that combine scholarly values with some degree of accessibility for the beginner. A few, such as Chomsky's *Syntactic Structures,* qualify much more strongly on the former count than on the latter, but have been included here because of their profound influence on the work of others. This handbook is intended to provide a grasp of broad outlines, a frame of reference, from which the more detailed and specific information may be considered and assimilated.

Linguists and teachers alike must realize that the teaching of English grammar in the schools is in a transition period that is confusing to both teachers and students. At the moment, teachers of English grammar cannot do full justice to their students without a thorough knowledge of traditional, structural, and transformational-generative approaches to the problems of analyzing the grammar of the English language. New textbooks show a variety of emphasis and many of the best are combinations of whatever the writer finds most useful in each of the three approaches. Because of the constantly shifting nature of our population, a single English class is apt to be made up of students who have a bewildering variety of previous training in English grammar. A teacher must be prepared to alienate the student by telling him to forget everything he has learned before and begin again, or be prepared to see and explain some connecting links between what he has learned and what he must now cope with. The latter course is easier on both student and teacher, but it can only be accomplished by a teacher who has knowledge of a variety of approaches to the problems of English grammar.

Trained linguists will find much to lament in the omissions made here. They are justly proud of the great strides made in their field and feel that justification of their feelings should be based only on the enormous amount of detailed study that supports these findings. We can only agree with them that a teacher whose background includes thorough training in linguistics is a better teacher of the language arts. But the overwhelming demands on a teacher's time and energy must also be recognized. Many teachers who teach the language arts must also teach history, geography, literature, art, music, mathematics, and elementary science. In addition they must put in several hours a week in pursuit of such nonscholarly occupations as "yard duty," attending faculty or Parents Club meetings, filling out the interminable forms required by this or that urgent school regulation, wiping noses, and instilling respect for the rights of others into the minds and hearts of their charges. While recognizing that linguistic research is a fascinating field, their most urgent concern is, understandably, how all this information can be reframed to elicit interest from the ten-year-old who evinces more concern for a ball of lint extracted from his jacket pocket than he shows for the workings of auxiliary verbs or the wondrously humanistic values to be found in consideration of his innate communicative skills.

Clearly, some bridges need to be built. This handbook is, then, an attempt at bridge-building.

San Rafael, California   J. H. H.
February 1970

ACKNOWLEDGMENTS

I should like to express my appreciation to those who have read all or part of this manuscript and offered helpful suggestions for its improvement. Any attempt to simplify tremendously complex material is most susceptible to the dangers of oversimplification. Thurston Womack of San Francisco State College fished me out of several such pitfalls, and Samuel Levin of Hunter College caught still other errors and misleading generalizations. Margaret Nearing of the Sacramento City College English Department contributed much to whatever understanding I possess of the problems of classroom teachers. This book owes a great deal to her straightforwardness, her total lack of pedagogical pomposity, and her kind encouragement. Among the elementary and secondary teachers who brought their classroom experience to a consideration of the manuscript and helped me to understand the audience I hope to reach were Gladys Baldwin, Katherine Blickhahn, Patrick F. Skinner, and Mary Ungersma. Many other teachers and soon-to-be teachers, who were students in my Modern Grammars classes at Dominican College and were, therefore, a practical proving ground for the early stages of the manuscript, contributed more than they know. They were so intent upon understanding what I told them—as opposed to just listening and taking notes to memorize—that they asked questions and pursued points until I was forced to frame my explanations as clearly and understandably as it was possible for me to do. Finally, there is my remarkable family, whose contributions are impossible to itemize or define. I cannot dedicate the book to Chuck, Mike, and Leanna; it is, in a very real sense, as much theirs as it is mine.

CONTENTS

A
SURVEY
OF
MODERN
GRAMMARS

PART ONE

CONTEXTS FOR
THE STUDY OF
MODERN GRAMMARS

SOME BASIC
CONSIDERATIONS

Before we take up a study of structural and generative grammars, it is well to begin with some orientation as to where we take up our study and some ideas as to the objectives we have in mind. Simplicity seems the best policy.

Man talks. He communicates his experience and thoughts, his hopes and fears to others; he transmits his accumulated knowledge to his children by means of oral sounds. Other men listen and comprehend. These facts are true of all communities of men, from the most primitive to the most sophisticated.

There are, of course, other means of communication. Hand signals, shrugs, nods, marks on paper, electrical dots and dashes, and smoke signals are a few of these. But the sounds made by man's vocal equipment are basic; the sounds and the patterns he forms with them are the raw materials of language.

Each language community has a set of mutually agreed upon methods for stringing together its sounds so that when one person speaks, another can be expected to understand what is said. Of the more than 3,000 languages known to exist in the world, only a comparative few have a written form of the language. Those that have no written form have, nevertheless, a grammatical system that is quite as complex as our own. Some systems are, in certain respects, even more complex. The fact that a language has a written form does not necessarily mean that its grammatical system is superior to the grammatical system of a language that has no written form. If a language is sufficient to the needs of those who use it, it is unrealistic to judge it by other criteria.

What is in the mind of man that enables him to organize his experience and thoughts into communicable form? No one knows. We only know that he does. And the organization is done in ways that are so highly complex that this ability alone sets mankind completely apart from all other life forms.

We do not know what is at the root of this ability, but its branches are all around us. We can take them apart and study them, classify them, compare them, and try to understand them.

The system of organization of any language is the grammar of that language. Various means may be used to analyze and sort out the grammar or system of any given language.

Most Americans are familiar with a grammatical analysis of English that is based on methods originated over 2,000 years ago. While it has the weight of all those years of scholarship behind it, it must be recognized that traditional means of grammatical analysis were developed to analyze classical Greek and Latin—both of which are quite different from modern English in several important ways. More recently, other methods have been developed for the analysis of languages, with specific means that allow for differences existing between languages. These means applied to the study of English have been further adapted to serve as educational materials in the elementary and secondary schools.

Among our objectives will be attempts to compare and contrast all these methods, not so much to choose "the best" as to understand the basic similarities and differences and to point out the strengths and weaknesses of each. This knowledge will enable us to understand the workings of Standard American English and to teach the language arts to elementary and secondary school students.

It is important that we grasp from the outset that these two specific areas of study exist side by side in the general field of language study. On the one hand, there is the attempt to understand man's ability to communicate and the means he employs to that end *for its own sake*. The roots of this study are found in the basic philosophical quest into the nature of knowledge itself. How do we know what we know? How do we organize our experience? How do we communicate with others? This study is sufficient unto itself for most modern linguistic scholars. These scholars bear a relationship to teachers of English that is analogous to the relationship of the research scientist to the general practitioner of medicine. One seeks information; the other seeks to apply that information to the more efficient handling of specific problems.

On the other hand, the teacher of English deals with the more immediate task of applying the findings of the language scholars to the training of the young in more effective and more efficient use of their innate language gifts. The teacher's task is one that the linguistic scholars are interested in—as they are interested in all facts of language and its use—but for the language scholars it does not loom so large in importance. The teacher is, by the same token, interested in language study but only as one facet of his primary function, which is to reach students as effectively as possible.

As we compare and contrast various methods used to analyze the grammar of the English language, we will look into the work of both the linguistic scholar and the English teacher. The orientation of each, the objectives, methods, and problems of each must be kept in mind at every stage of the inquiry.

Ideally, those who wish to gain something worthwhile from a comparative study of this kind should have a background that includes a solid working knowledge of anthropology, at least one or two languages other than English, the history and development of the English language, and the history of linguistic study as it has evolved over the past 2,000 years. This ideal set of qualifications rarely exists. What can we do about it?

Perhaps if we examine what each of these areas of study can contribute to an understanding of modern linguistic study, we can find means to fill in some of the missing pieces.

Anthropology, according to the *American College Dictionary,* is "the science that treats of the origin, development (physical, intellectual, moral, etc.), and varieties, and sometimes especially the cultural development, customs, beliefs, etc., of mankind." Such a study would provide, as nothing else could, a broad awareness of the fact that all men may look out upon the same world but that they do not view that world from the same window. The differences that do exist in the highly varied interpretations of what is seen from all those other windows can be contrasted for a far better appreciation and understanding of our own.

A knowledge of another language or languages is of prime importance. No collection of random examples can serve to point out how very different various languages are in their structure. Knowledge of two or more complete systems, even though the languages may be closely related, makes differences of grammatical structure a part of the student's awareness—not something he must be persuaded to believe.

It is most important that the student know something of the ways in which English developed. Students of the structure of modern English should know that English began with the Germanic dialects brought to the British islands 1,500 years ago. They should know something of the major influences of Latin and French, and of the minor influences of the Celtic and Scandinavian languages. They should know of the rapid changes in the structure of the language during the two centuries following the Norman Conquest when French was the language of the upper classes and of written record in England and English survived primarily as a spoken language, and of some of the changes brought about by other political, economic, and social factors. They should know, too, the conditions under which the traditional rules of "correctness" were established for the Standard British English and Standard American English of today. In addition to the wealth of information this provides about our own language, it demonstrates most vividly the fact that any language spoken by living people may also be recognized as a "living" thing. Living things, by their very nature, change—and language is no exception.

Finally, those who know something of the history of linguistic study will be aware of the basis for traditional methods and objectives of language analysis. They will be better able to compare these methods and objectives with those of modern linguistic analysis. Mere knowledge of the rules of traditional grammar is not enough. The student should know what lies behind those rules—who established them and how and why—before he can make an intelligent comparison with modern approaches.

This knowledge of the history of linguistic study will also provide an awareness that the application of scientific method to the investigation of how languages grow, develop, and work is not new but has a foundation of respected scholarship that stretches back over the past two centuries. The "New English" is new only to the elementary and secondary schools.

Some of the discussion of these topics will seem to stray rather far afield from our purpose, the study of modern grammars. As we continue, their relevance and significance will become apparent.

TWO THOUSAND YEARS OF LANGUAGE STUDY

When one human being communicates with another by means of spoken language, it can safely be assumed that several distinct events have occurred. These are:

1. An ideational stimulus to the mind of the speaker
2. The formulation of a language statement by the speaker
3. The physical act of speaking
4. Sound waves in the atmosphere
5. The physical process of hearing
6. The mental sorting of the language statement by the hearer
7. Understanding the idea by the hearer

There are those who argue that the first two of these are so closely interrelated that they constitute a single event. The same argument is often given for considering the final two items to be a single event. It is not necessary to settle this dispute for our purposes. For the moment, let us arbitrarily settle upon the seven items or events above as a touchstone for the discussion of how language scholars have approached the problems of analyzing and describing the language around them.

TRADITIONAL GRAMMAR THEORY

The Greeks

The earliest known efforts of Western man to analyze the phenomena of language dealt only with steps one and two above.

Plato began by searching for the source of man's knowledge. There were, he thought, universal truths, universal ideas, that lay behind the language of the Greeks. He did not consider that other languages were in any way worthy of study or consideration; they were barbaric. The Greeks spoke several dialects but these, in Plato's view, were simply decayed or degenerate versions of a once-perfect system of communication.

Things thought about and spoken of and what was thought or said of them were not matters to be considered in the narrow light of grammatical forms and relationships but matters of detail in the much broader study of the thought processes by which man—Greek man— organized his experience, established relationships of ideas, drew conclusions, and made judgments. Plato treated matters that are, today, a part of the fields of philosophy, psychology, rhetoric, and semantics, as well as grammar. Man's knowledge and his ability to communicate with his fellows were a single, rich field of inquiry.

In order to pick out Plato's ideas on the limited subject of grammar, it is necessary to take them out of a much broader context. He spoke of *onoma,* or the name of one who performs an action, and *rhēma,* the name of an action, and the relationships of the ideas or meanings expressed by each. He felt that there were acceptable ways to express ideas and that deviation from these acceptable ways was clearly wrong. This belief in universality permeated his thinking to the point that, in the *Cratylus* dialogue, one of Plato's speakers argued for the belief that there was a valid relationship between words and the things or actions that they identified. He meant, of course, good Greek words.

Aristotle believed that debate on this point was absurd. He insisted that language was arrived at by convention and agreement of the speakers of a given language. For example, *aēr,* the Greek word for *air,* was not based on some innate airiness of the sounds, but was simply a combination of sounds arbitrarily agreed upon among Greeks to express the notion of air.

It was Aristotle who initiated the use of the term *syndesmoi* to designate those words that did not fall into the *onoma* and *rhēma,* or noun and verb categories, but were used primarily to link nouns and verbs together in grammatical constructions. The English translation for the word is *conjunction,* but Aristotle used it to apply to all words other than nouns and verbs.

Somewhat later, in the great learning center of Alexandria, a scholar named Dionysius Thrax pulled all the fragmented ideas about Greek grammar into a single short work called *The Art of Grammar.* Written in the first century B.C., the grammar was only about 400 lines long and yet for twenty centuries it has influenced the work of countless grammarians in the formulation of grammars for virtually all the languages of Europe.

The Art of Grammar divided the Greek language into eight parts of speech—noun, verb, participle, article, pronoun, preposition, adverb, and conjunction—defined these in a variety of ways, and outlined the uses of each in sentences. Consideration was also given to letters and to syllables since, to Thrax and his contemporaries, language study meant the study of *written* language and the conventions of correctness established by great writers.

The Greeks established for the world of language study the first terminology for discussing their subject; they established the practice of analyzing written representations of human speech which was to become one of the hallmarks of traditional grammatical investigation and evaluation; and, finally, they established as a basic assumption the idea that there was a universally correct and acceptable logic of language for man to follow in expressing his ideas.

The Romans

The Romans imitated the Greeks in linguistic matters as they did in many other areas of culture and learning. Some Romans, notably Julius Caesar and Quintilian, the rhetorician, raised questions of how far language scholars could go in setting up rules for the logic of language which differed from the way that the language was used by most of its speakers. This gap between scholarly rule and common usage widened into the distinct difference between the Latin of classical literature and the Vulgar (here meaning common) Latin spoken by the masses of Roman people. Still, the most influential works written on the grammar of Latin were to follow the pattern established by Thrax in writing of Greek.

The early standard Latin grammar was that written by Marcus Varro in the first century. A later work written by Priscian in the sixth century consisted of eighteen books on parts of speech and two on syntax. This was to be the basis for standard Latin grammars throughout medieval times when Latin was the international language of the learned.

It is important to note that the rigidly categorized parts of speech were notionally defined in some cases—as with the noun and verb—and described according to their function in others—as with the preposition and conjunction. Latin grammarians found it necessary to adjust the eight parts of speech decreed for Greek. Latin had no articles, but since the Greeks had dictated that any self-respecting language had eight parts of speech, Latin grammarians replaced the category for articles with one for interjections. An extensive list of inflections had to be listed and classified for each part of speech. Conjugations and declensions were mandatory since the inflectional ending contained a part of the meaning of most words. For example, endings added to nouns indicated whether the noun was subject of the verb, direct or indirect object, the means of accomplishing the action, the result of an action, and so on. Verbs had literally dozens of inflectional endings. Each one signified some combination of person, number, tense, and mood. Every inflectional ending had to be categorized and defined; rules had to be established for the use of each and exceptions noted. The order in which words appeared in a sentence was of comparatively little importance since any nominal or verbal elements were clearly labeled with their function in the sentence by whatever inflectional endings they carried.

The Romans bowed to Greek precedent in setting up the grammatical rules for their language, and the practice spread with the Empire and, later, with the Church over all of Europe.

The medieval period

Because Latin was the language of Church scholarship and of serious literature all through the Middle Ages, the vernaculars—the languages of the masses of uneducated people—that were to become the Romance languages, grew and developed without rules other than those established by usage and custom. Still, these languages were of Latin origin and when, with the rise of nationalism, each country felt the need of its own scholarly grammar, it was a comparatively easy task to fit these languages into the mold fashioned for classical Greek and modified slightly for classical Latin.

Among scholars, great emphasis was placed on orderly argumentation and logic, so it is not surprising that grammatical rules were held valid only when they adhered to logical system. Those who established rules for these languages made them adhere to strictly formulated logical principles dictated by Latin scholarship rather than attempting to fathom the logic or system that had developed as a part of each language.

England

In England, too, classical grammatical concepts were brought to bear by those who sought to establish standards of usage for a language that had become a symbol of national identity and pride.

England was to have no language academy as did several other countries, but in the eighteenth century a number of influential men of letters and school masters began to have a regularizing effect on some of England's writers and, to a far greater degree, on her schools. It was an age marked by great reverence for the classical—in literature, art, architecture, even matters of fashion—and so it was natural that the grammarians sought the status of a classically correct grammar for their language.

The dictionary of Samuel Johnson and the school grammars of John Wallis, Robert Lowth, and Lindley Murray were not only aimed at establishing "correct" usage but at pointing out "errors." Their criteria for such decisions were often based upon a familiarity with the requirements of Latin grammar, which was secure in its centuries of scholarly prestige, rather than upon serious consideration of the somewhat different grammatical system used by native speakers of the English language.

The task of forcing English into the Latin grammar mold was doubly difficult because English is not derived from Latin but from old Germanic dialects. Undaunted by differences, these eighteenth-century grammarians equated English auxiliary verbs with Latin verb inflections and endowed English with a complete future tense and an almost totally alien subjunctive mood among other things. They forced the modal system derived from the Germanic into a variety of Latin categories. *Shall* and *will* became a part of the future tense; *may* became a part of the subjunctive mood. The Lowth and Murray grammars were the most widely used in England for several generations. Their pronouncements on matters of English grammar set standards of usage that left an indelible mark on the language itself.

These grammarians are often called *prescriptive grammarians* because their objectives were largely those of establishing rules to be taught to young students and by which literary efforts might be judged, at least in part.

COMPARATIVE AND HISTORICAL LINGUISTICS

In spite of the fact that most grammarians relied upon classical grammarians for method and classical languages for criteria of correctness, some new ideas were stirring in the field of language study in the eighteenth century. These new ideas were not to affect the work of school grammarians for several generations. But among these ideas are to be found the roots of a whole new approach to the problem of analyzing and describing language.

Many language scholars had noted similarities between various European languages; some languages had quite clearly developed from one variety or another of provincial Latin. It remained for an Englishman who was not primarily a language scholar to see relationships among the most widely dispersed of those languages which were later to be recognized as the Indo-European family of languages.

Sir William Jones had served in the colonial government of India and while there had studied Sanskrit. In 1786 he wrote of observing similarities between a remarkable number of vocabulary items in Sanskrit and their equivalents in European and Middle Eastern languages. He suggested that all these languages might have "sprung from some common source, which, perhaps, no longer exists."

Investigation of similarities and differences among languages is called *comparative linguistics*. As language scholars began to establish patterns of relationships among languages, their work came to be called *historical linguistics*. (These scholars were interested primarily in relationships among languages; they were concerned with matters of grammar only insofar as these might indicate relationships among languages and not as a matter of establishing rules of correctness.) Their research was simply a matter of gathering data, sorting and analyzing it. Their view of change was totally objective. They were only interested in what kinds of changes had occurred, not whether these changes were "right" or "wrong," "good" or "bad."

After two centuries of enormous amounts of language study, linguists have arrived at some very sweeping theories about the nature of the relationships among the many Indo-European languages. Stated in the simplest possible terms, the important points are these: (1) All these languages developed from a single language which no longer exists. (2) Differences developed when groups of people who spoke this language moved apart and were separated for long periods of time. That is, one group moved into India and their language developed and changed to become Sanskrit; another group moved into southeastern Europe and their language grew into the ancestor of Greek; another group broke off and moved into northern Europe and their language changed in some respects to become the parent language of German, English, Danish and so on. (3) The fact that all these languages share a common heritage accounts for the fact that some similarities still exist in all of them.

Among the first linguists to make important comparative studies was a Danish scholar named Rasmus Rask, who compared Icelandic and Scandinavian languages and dialects. Another, Jacob Grimm, carried Rask's studies still further and proposed a theory to account for the differences he found among languages. Out of these and many other, similar studies grew the theory that languages not only change gradually, over long periods of time, but that they change systematically and that the changes are best traced through comparison of the sound systems of languages.

The single most sweeping statement of this kind of sound relationship is often referred to as Grimm's Law or the First Germanic Consonant Shift. It is a systematic comparison of the sound systems of Indo-European languages which both demonstrates the validity of the theory that these languages sprang from a common source and gives a wealth of information about how they are related.

Grimm concentrated, as had his predecessors, on written forms of words. Actually, he had no choice since he dealt with stages of language development long past. The differences he noted and compared were letters and spellings, but the spelling differences came to be recognized as representative of pronunciation or sound differences. Grimm went even further and, in addition to a simple listing and comparing of differences, he proposed an explanation of the orderly nature of the shift.

According to this theory, whole sets of sounds in an ancestor of the Germanic languages had shifted from their earlier Indo-European pronunciation. The voiced stop consonants *b, d,* and *g* had shifted or changed to voiceless stop consonants *p, t,* and *k*. During the same period, sounds that had begun as the voiceless stop consonants *p, t,* and *k* changed to voiceless spirants (sounds produced by constricting but not completely stopping the flow of air) *f, th,* and *h*. A third set of sounds, which had begun as the aspirated stops *bh, dh,* and *gh* in early stages of Indo-European language development and still remain in Sanskrit, had developed into similar, but not quite the same, sounds *ph* or *f, th,* and *h* in later stages of Indo-European language development represented by Latin and Greek. As a part of the Germanic Consonant Shift, this group of sounds shifted to become the voiced stop consonant *b, d,* and *g*. The shift of all three sets of consonant sounds—for speakers of the Germanic parent language only—can be seen as something very like a game of phonetic musical chairs.

CHART OF THE FIRST GERMANIC CONSONANT SHIFT

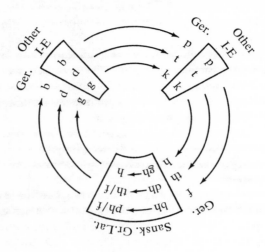

The boxed letters represent the sounds that remained in other Indo-European languages; the letters outside the boxes represent the sounds found in Germanic languages as a result of the consonant shift. These correspondences figure prominently in setting the languages derived from this Germanic parent language apart as a distinct branch of the Indo-European family of languages.

These shifts, to repeat, occurred gradually, over very long periods of time. They can be demonstrated by comparing words in a Germanic language, English, which developed after the shifts occurred, with items taken from Latin and Greek, languages in which the sounds of these consonants did not shift.

	English		*English*		*English*
Latin	*turba* → *thorp*	Greek	*pous* → *foot*	Greek	*phrater* → *brother*
Latin	*dentum* → *tooth*	Greek	*treis* → *three*	Greek	*thygater* → *daughter*
Greek	*agros* → *acre*	Latin	*cor* → *heart*	Latin	*hostis* → *guest*

Many words in these languages do not show precisely the same correspondences, but these can be shown to be the result of other shifts or to be related to other factors. Scholars such as Karl Verner noted additional complexities in the nature of the shift and differences resulting from later shifts and proposed theories to explain the apparent "exceptions," until it was possible to trace, in great detail, the development of Indo-European languages over vast stretches of history.

More language samples were gathered, examined, and analyzed; more comparisons were made and new theories proposed. Each new theory could be tested by gathering still more language data and making still more comparisons.

The area of inquiry had been greatly expanded with investigation of Sanskrit and the languages of the Middle East. Sanskrit provided an especially rich body of material for these historical linguists because of the nature of the records open to them. Sanskrit, a literary language of India, had been the subject of grammatical study centuries before Western European scholars had undertaken such investigation of their own languages. As early as the fourth century B.C., an Indian grammarian named Pānini had analyzed Sanskrit and had organized his analysis into a masterful codification of the grammatical units and possible combinations in Sanskrit. For students of historical linguistics, discovery and study of this work was profoundly valuable for two reasons. First, it was a full-fledged grammatical analysis as compared to the fragmentary records of some of the earlier languages they had studied and, second, it represented by far the earliest stage of development of any Indo-European language available to them for study.

Through most of the nineteenth century, linguistic scholarship concentrated primarily on comparative and historical studies. Methods of gathering, classifying and analyzing data were tested, improved, or discarded, and the improvements tested again.

Comparison of the sound systems of languages was seen to account for only a part of the systematic changes in language. Word forms, inflections, and syntactic differences came to be recognized as important considerations in comparing different stages of the development of languages.

This study of the historical development of a language or languages is sometimes called *diachronic linguistics. Diachronic* is a combination of Greek stems, *dia-* meaning *across* and *chronos* meaning *time.* For linguists it means that single features of language are traced over long periods of time with changes noted and related to changes in other features of languages over the same periods.

Language researchers gathered data from every nook and cranny of Europe including many dialects peculiar to very small, isolated villages and hamlets. This data led to a major shift of emphasis for some linguists. From the study of historical developments, they moved into primary concentration on the similarities and contrasts between contemporary languages and dialects.

Those who concentrated on contemporary language differences began to develop their own methodologies and to define more clearly their areas of investigation. This new branch of language study came to be called *synchronic linguistics. Synchronic* is a combination of the Greek *syn-* meaning *together* and *chronos.* For linguists it means those features of language existing together in time. Synchronic linguistics looks neither forward nor backward but concentrates upon all the systems, relationships and means of communicating ideas in a given language at a given point in time.

Some linguistic scholars believed that the methods shown to be successful in historical—or diachronic—studies could be adapted to use in synchronic research. These linguists also believed that such analysis of contemporary languages would lead to greater insights into precisely how languages worked.

Other scholars believed that synchronic linguistics presented problems that were very different from those presented by historical studies, and that different methods were, therefore, required.

Among the most influential of those who sought methods that could claim scientific rigor and, at the same time, be specifically designed for the task of synchronic analysis was Ferdinand de Saussure, a Swiss-born Frenchman, who worked and taught at the University of Geneva at the turn of the century.

De Saussure believed that linguistic changes come about over such very long periods of time that scholars were perfectly free to ignore such changes in investigating a language at a single stage of its development. He recognized that every speaker of a language is likely to show some individual differences in the way that he uses his language. But even so, he said, certain conventions are agreed upon by the members of a speech community. That is, the language habits of each member of a language community may differ in some ways from the habits of other members of the community but there is still a considerable area of overlapping. This area of overlap contains all those linguistic signals and notions that each member of the speech community shares with all of the others. This common area may exist only in abstract form; each member of the community may deviate in some ways; but all must operate within the common base to a great extent.

He assigned the term *parole* to the diverse practices of individual speakers of a language and the term *langue* to the area of overlap—the linguistic principles adhered to, however unconsciously, by *all* members of a speech community. Obviously, *la langue* is an abstraction. It was the business of the synchronic linguist, thought de Saussure, to investigate and analyze *la langue*.

These ideas were crucial to delimiting an area of study for the synchronic linguist. They relieved him of attention to historical change and variation; they relieved him of attention to multitudes of minor individual differences; they focused his attention on the heart of the problem—the facts of language agreed upon or shared by the members of a language community at a given point in time. Obviously the existence of historic and individual differences was a recognized fact but, as far as the synchronic linguistic investigator was concerned, such differences were put firmly in their place and labeled.

De Saussure's brilliant linguistic insights also included consideration of the troublesome problem of the boundary between ideation and the measurable area of human speech. Quite simply he believed the two to be inextricably bound together. A linguistic sign—whatever communicates from speaker to hearer—is made up of two interacting parts, the notional meaning and the combinations of sound used to give that meaning linguistic life. In short, semantics and grammar are two faces of a coin. Slice the coin in half and neither portion has legitimate value. Each portion might be examined separately but examination of one side of the coin does not constitute examination of the coin.

Others shared de Saussure's conviction that grammarians should broaden their area of inquiry to include all the steps of the communicative process—or at least steps one through four.

In addition to broad grammatical concerns, grammarians such as Henry Sweet and Otto Jespersen placed great emphasis on the analysis of sounds used by speakers of English to communicate their thoughts. They saw that commonly used English spelling was an unacceptable means of representing the speech sounds made by speakers of English. Henry Sweet led the way for English grammarians seeking to establish a system of representing speech sounds with the greatest possible fidelity to their spoken form. The key requirement for such a system is that each symbol represent one and only one sound. Sweet's phonetic alphabet, like those proposed by other language scholars, placed greatest emphasis on the physical means of sound production. Consideration was given to such factors as whether a sound involved resonance or not, the parts of the vocal equipment—lips, tongue, teeth, and so on—shaping the sound, the degree to which the flow of air was constricted and the factors of lip-rounding or tenseness involved.

Grammarians dealing with English from the time of Sweet onward have been influenced to some degree by his work.

Traditional grammarians—and these included Sweet himself—still worked within the classical framework established for defining parts of speech and syntactic devices used by a speech community to communicate ideational or notional meaning. In addition, they began to add investigation of the sound systems of languages to their field of study. They worked from both the standpoint of the notional meaning and from the standpoint of the sound system of the language. The main framework of their analysis still rested on its traditional foundations but they recognized that speakers of English expressed their ideas in ways that were unique to English in some respects. They saw that matters of syntax and word order were more important to the grammar of English and the proportion of their work devoted to syntactic analysis increased accordingly.

They still attempted to sort the English language into parts of speech and syntactic functions by defining logical—or psychological— meanings expressed by speakers of English. Definitions of parts of speech still listed referents and syntactic function or meaning as well as accidence (the forms taken by a given part of speech). For example, nouns were the names of persons, places, states, qualities and other "things"; they served as subjects, objects, complements, and so on; and they showed singular and plural number and had a common and a genitive case.

Many English words and classes of words do not fit as neatly into this kind of classification as nouns. Some, such as prepositions, do not vary in form; some, such as *man, fancy, ship,* and *paint,* skip nimbly from one part of speech category to another; and some, such as gerunds, have the notional characteristics of more than one part of speech.

Consideration of syntactic or contextual characteristics presented these grammarians with even greater problems. Syntactic structures and functions do not lend themselves readily to simple, easily memorized notional definitions because English word order allows such an enormous range of distributional possibilities. Simply listing the possibilities is a formidable task; attempting to explain them in terms of what each means is an undertaking of staggering proportions. Those works that even approached a complete description of the grammar of English were the seven-volume work of Otto Jespersen and the five-volume work of Hendrik Poutsma.

While these lengthy works contain analysis of enormous quantities of examples and variations in the use of English, they are still open to criticism on the grounds that rigorously controlled methods of defini- tion occasionally lapse into intuitive or "common sense" definition. This becomes especially troublesome when exceptions to a "rule" are at least as numerous and commonplace among speakers of the language as instances of compliance with the rule. For example, the future tense was said to be expressed by the use of the forms *shall* and *will* but English speakers are just as likely to indicate futurity by means of ad- verbs as in "The play opens tomorrow." Another thing that the ex- haustive volume of traditional analysis did not obscure was the fact that the fundamental definitions were still, in many instances, circular. For example, a sentence was defined as a group of words expressing a complete thought and containing a subject and a predicate; subject and predicate were defined as being necessary parts of sentences. These definition problems still present difficulties for traditional grammarians.

DESCRIPTIVE AND STRUCTURAL LINGUISTICS

Impatient with the many factors that relied so heavily on subjective evaluation and classification, the definitions that were impossible to verify except intuitively, and the voluminous work that seemed inevitably circular and at times self-contradictory, many linguistic scholars began to direct their attention almost exclusively to events in the communicative process that could be considered objectively—the articulation of language sounds by the speaker, the sound waves produced, and human hearing. These sounds and the systematic combinations made of them are the observable data of language.

Those who hoped to eliminate the problems of the traditional grammarians and establish more rigorous means of classification and analysis by concentrating on the measurable events in the communicative process argued that linguistic scientists cannot investigate that which they cannot see or measure and this obviously includes ideation and notional meaning. In language study, they believed, they could only work toward examination of notional meaning by examining the objectively verifiable events of speech and the physical situations in which an utterance appears—the situation in which it is spoken and the observable response that it elicits.

American linguistics

From this point on, our discussion will concentrate upon American linguistics. This is not to minimize the work of modern European linguistics but to simplify our discussion.

In America in the early part of the twentieth century, great strides in linguistics were linked with anthropological research as Franz Boas and, later, Edward Sapir and others brought new methods to the study of American Indian languages. In dealing with languages that had no written form, and, more importantly, languages that were cast in the molds of often radically different ways of organizing human experience, Boas saw that the grammatical categories of Indo-European languages simply could not be adjusted to fit. The verbs in American Indian languages, for example, might have no system of tense. The concepts of time might be classified as a part of human reaction, memory or expectation, absence of an occurrence from the field of vision, and so on.

Boas proposed that the overall system of a given language might be analyzed as three subsystems: first, the individual sounds used by the speakers of a language; second, the categories of meaning units made up of sound combinations; and third, the systems of combining these units of meaning to communicate complex ideas and experiences. Because Boas and others who used similar methods sought to describe languages as they were used instead of fitting them into an already established grammatical pattern, their field became known as *descriptive linguistics.* Because descriptive methods became the basis for analysis of the structure of English and other languages, the term *structural linguistics* came into general use.

Independent of reference to classical language categories, working with languages that had developed without authoritarian rules for "correct" usage, Sapir found the dozen and a half Indian languages he analyzed to be beautifully systematic and orderly. His attention to detail and his sense of wonder at the communicative skills of man were to inspire a vigorous and exciting period in linguistics in America.

Still another American, Leonard Bloomfield, is widely regarded as the father of linguistics in this country. Where Sapir and others had considered mental process a part of their legitimate area of inquiry, Bloomfield defined the scientific study of language as one that admitted only data which could be objectively verified. It was he who drew the line that not only emphasized the importance of observable events in human communication but virtually ruled out the others as beyond the scope of scientific research. His *Language,* published in 1933, is still considered the single most influential work in the field of descriptive linguistics ever printed in this country. It is a comprehensive, detailed statement of the principles of a scientific approach to linguistic research. The role of the scientific linguist is defined as consisting of gathering data, classifying, analyzing, and describing it.

Other language scholars maintained that meaning was a primary concern of those who would study language, but structuralist or descriptive method came to be more and more respected and for several decades the views expressed by Bloomfield were the most widely accepted in the field of language study. Descriptive methods are still being refined and applied to the analysis of many of the world's languages. They are particularly useful and effective in the study of African, Indian, Polynesian and other languages that exist only in spoken form.

In the years during and immediately after World War II, Charles Fries and others worked with descriptive analyses of languages in training military personnel and their methods proved remarkably effective. Fries also made a serious attempt to bring scientific descriptive methods to the study of modern American English. His *American English Grammar,* published in 1940, was an analysis of contemporary American language habits based on the analysis of a collection of letters made available to him by the United States government. In 1952 he published *The Structure of English,* which was based on an analysis of some 250,000 words of spoken language, using recorded telephone conversa-

tions as a corpus. In order to free his word categories from precon-
ceptions associated with traditional grammatical terminology, Fries assigned numbers and letters to word categories—a practice still followed
in some school texts.

Others, bringing structural methods to bear on the problem of
analyzing American English, published even more carefully detailed
works that retained the method of dividing their analysis into three
levels—phonology, the sound system; morphology, the system of meaningful grammatical units or combinations of sound; and syntax, the
system of combining morphological units into larger structures. George
Trager and Henry Lee Smith, Jr., did influential work in describing
the sound system of English. Archibald A. Hill and Nelson Francis
published widely used structural analyses of American English for use
as college texts in modern English grammar. James Sledd attempted
to combine the best of traditional and structural methods by retaining
some traditional definitions based on meaning while making use of
many of the findings of structural linguistics particularly in the matters
of the sound system and establishment of word categories. These books,
together with others of similar nature, and large numbers of shorter
works and articles in language and education periodicals began to bridge
the gap between linguist and teacher.

GENERATIVE OR TRANSFORMATIONAL THEORY

Still another approach to the problem of analyzing the grammar
of English grew out of the work of Zellig Harris, a structuralist who
hoped that linguistic research could go a step beyond classification and
description to arrive at some far-reaching theories about the distributional regularities and logic of languages. One of his followers, Noam
Chomsky, was particularly challenged by this proposal.

In 1957 Chomsky published *Syntactic Structures* in which he discussed several possible methods of theorizing about the syntactic regularities of the English language and suggested the one he felt most likely
to meet requirements of simplicity and precision while at the same time
dealing with the staggering complexity and creativity of the language.
Briefly, the preferred theory involved various formulas or rules for
describing simple declarative English sentences and demonstrating relationships holding between the parts of the sentences. A second set of
formulas or rules would be required for transforming these into other
types of sentences and structures. The theory has undergone some altera-
tion and a good deal of elaboration in the years since but the basic
premise remains unchanged.

Since the theory seeks to set up a system that will generate sentences, it is frequently called *generative grammar*. Because a part of the theory involves transforming basic sentence types into other types such as questions and negative and passive sentences, and so on, it is sometimes called *transformational grammar*. Generative refers to the objective of the system while transformation is a part of the process. Occasionally it is referred to by the combined term *transformational-generative grammar*.

The system assumes that sentences such as

> Michael didn't paint the portrait.
> Did Michael paint the portrait?
> What did Michael paint?
> The portrait was painted by Michael.

are all based on transformations of a single simple, declarative sentence, "Michael painted the portrait." All of the sentences, then, have several basic, underlying meanings and grammatical relationships in common. Each of the sentences above has a different appearance. On the surface they are different sentences. But, given the phrase structure and transformational rules of generative grammar, their underlying similarities can be demonstrated effectively. The differences in the appearance of the sentences "Michael painted the portrait" and "The portrait was painted by Michael" are said to be differences of *surface structure* only. The meanings and relationships that hold between the parts of these two sentences are the same. These underlying meanings are said to represent the *deep structure* of the two sentences.

Without ever having seen a transformational-generative formula— or any other kind of traditional or structural description, for that matter —a native speaker of English would immediately agree that the example sentences above have a great deal in common. While at a loss to explain with precision exactly *what* they have in common, the native speaker knows that they are, in some way, "talking about the same thing." Somewhere in his mental apparatus is stored a knowledge of the grammar of his language—the "rules" of putting English sounds and words together in meaningful combinations. This same intuitive knowledge enables him to determine immediately whether a string of sounds or symbols constitute an English sentence or not. He knows that "Michael did not paint the portrait" is a sentence in English. He knows that "portrait Michael paint not the did" is a string of English words but that the string does not constitute an English sentence.

The native speaker's knowledge of how the language works— whether he can *explain* how it works or not—is called his *competence* by the generative grammarian. The native speaker's production of

English sentences may falter occasionally if he is rushed or excited or tired, he may absent-mindedly produce a sentence that will cause confusion in the mind of another native speaker, but the fact that his *performance* may have its flaws does not mean that a basic competence is not present. When that same individual walks across a room, he may stumble if he is rushed or excited or tired, but that does not mean that he does not know how to walk.

Generative grammar borrows from both traditional and structural approaches to grammatical analysis. It reverts to the traditional position that mental process is the legitimate concern of the language scholar and it seeks to describe the intuitive grammatical knowledge of native speakers of a language. At the same time it makes use of the vast amount of research done by structuralists, and its criteria for grammaticality are based on evidence as to how the language is actually used rather than prescribing rules for correctness based on the supposedly superior grammatical system or logic of some other language.

Chomsky has drawn fire from some structuralists for blurring the edges of what they regard as their strictly scientific discipline and from others for the difficulty of dealing with the formula approach he finds most effective in describing the underlying system of the vast number of grammatically correct sentences possible in English.

Those who find his theory useful and productive argue that scientists in other fields theorize beyond their known data as a matter of course and that the problems of dealing with the generative formulas are largely a matter of their being new and unfamiliar.

A more serious charge is brought by those who contend that the generative grammarians may, in their quest for a complete description of the language, become rigidly prescriptive in their rule-making and describe a grammatical system that does not allow for the great variety of dialects in the English language or for the gradually changing nature of a living language.

In their purest form the formulas are quite complex—particularly those dealing with the knottier problems of deep structure—but several adaptations, notably those by Paul Roberts and Ralph Goodman, are far less intimidating to classroom teachers and their students.

The scholarly conflict between the structuralists and the generative grammar theorists has served as a spur to both camps and the field of language study has, as a result, entered a most vigorous and challenging era.

3

A SUMMARY
OF THE HISTORY
OF THE ENGLISH LANGUAGE

Our investigation of modern grammars will deal only with English. Much of what we study will be more easily grasped if we know something of how the language came to be what it is today. There is, obviously, no point in either time or space that can be designated as the specific point at which English began. Most of those who write of the history of the English language settle upon the geographic location of what is now England and discuss the speech of the peoples who have lived there.

The language that we speak today is derived from a collection of Germanic dialects—sometimes called Teutonic dialects—that were first brought to the English islands in the fourth and fifth centuries. These grew into the dialects now referred to as Old English. Just when did they cease to be Germanic dialects and become Old English dialects? Again, geographic location is the decisive factor. When these settlers came to English shores, their language is considered to be Old English and thus the beginning date for the language is set at about A.D. 450.

Since we know that such decisions are arbitrary, it will be well to know something of the ancestry of these dialects and their relationship to other languages.

The 3,000 or so languages of the world can be grouped into about 300 language families on the basis of similarities in their basic word stock and grammar. One of these families, the Indo-European, is made up of most of the languages of Europe, the Near East and India. Among these is English.

The prehistoric Indo-European parent language, which can only be reconstructed by studying the languages derived from it, was probably very highly inflected. That is, it was a language in which the various forms of a given word show its relationship to other words in a sentence. When groups of speakers of this language moved away from the original homeland—believed to be somewhere in the easternmost part of Europe—the language of each group grew and developed along different lines in much the same way that American and Australian English now show differences from the language of England. Over very long periods of complete isolation from each other, these dialects of a single language changed so much that they became separate languages —the speakers of one were unintelligible to speakers of another. Further population shifts resulted in still other divisions and subdivisions into other languages.

One major branch of the Indo-European language family is called Italic, from which Latin and, later, the Romance languages developed. Another is called Germanic, which is the linguistic ancestor of English. These relationships are charted on pages 26–27.

The earliest known languages of England

The first peoples known to inhabit the land that was later to become England were Celts. Their languages were dialects of still another branch of the Indo-European language family.

The second major language known in England was the Latin of Roman Legions. The fierce, blue-painted Celtic warriors threw off the initial attempt made to add their lands to the Roman Empire in 55–54 B.C., but a century later they were overwhelmed by a much larger Roman army. Most of the island of Britain was occupied by Roman Legions, government officials and their households from about A.D. 43 until about 410. When the Empire began to crumble, the military and governing officials withdrew, abandoning an elaborate system of roads and many settlements built around the installations of a military government. These bore such names as Lancaster, Doncaster, Worcester, and Gloucester—all derived in part from the Latin word *castra,* or camp.

THE OLD ENGLISH PERIOD a.d. 450–1066

The Germanic Angles, Saxons, and Jutes

The withdrawal of Roman troops virtually invited the invasion of the rich lowlands by the Picts and Scots from the north. The Celts ap-

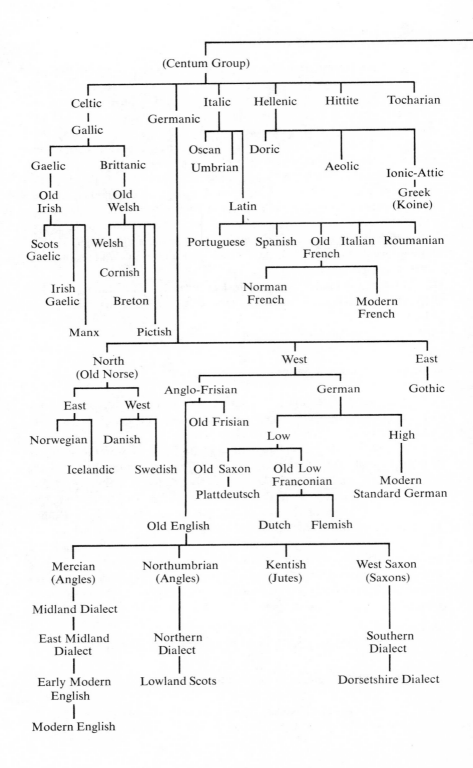

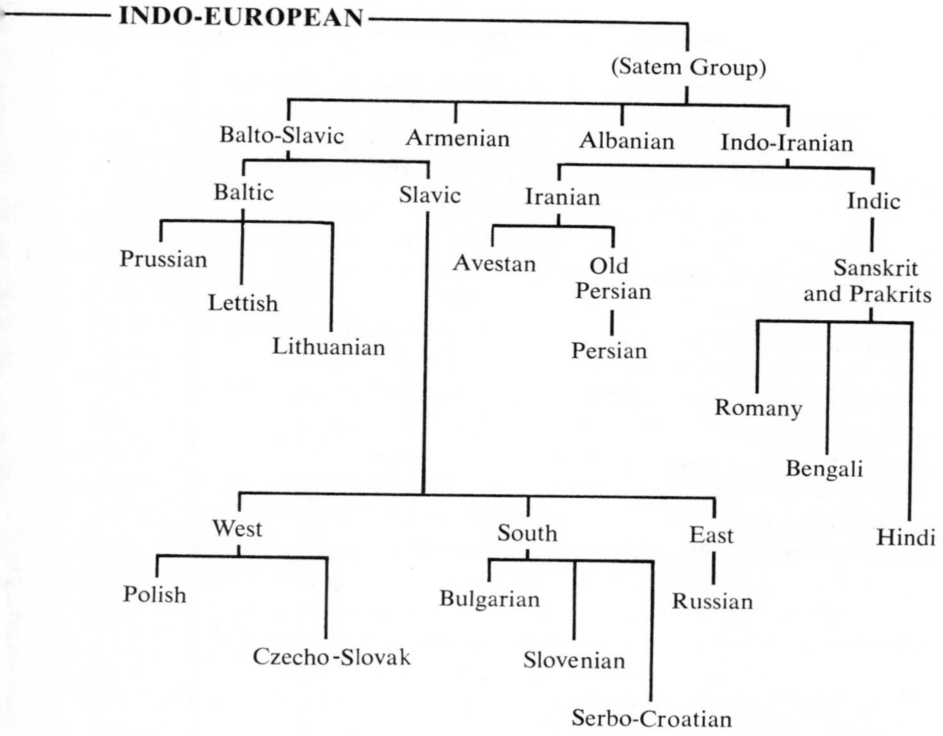

INDO-EUROPEAN

(Satem Group)

Balto-Slavic Armenian Albanian Indo-Iranian

Baltic Slavic Iranian Indic

Prussian

Lettish

Lithuanian

Avestan Old Persian

Persian

Sanskrit and Prakrits

Romany

Bengali

Hindi

West South East

Polish

Czecho-Slovak

Bulgarian Russian

Slovenian

Serbo-Croatian

RELATIONSHIPS OF SOME

INDO-EUROPEAN LANGUAGES

with

DETAIL OF ENGLISH DIALECTS

pealed to some settlers new to their shores—bands of Jutes from across the North Sea—for aid in defending their land. Soon the Jutes and other Germanic tribes called Angles and Saxons came in greater and greater numbers. The Celts found too late that their new allies had become their conquerors. Although wars of resistance continued for the next 200 years, the Celtic peoples were pushed steadily north and west or across the English Channel to French Brittany or remained to be subjected to the rule of the newcomers.

These Germanic tribes took permanent control of the land that was later to be called England. Their language dominated and almost totally blotted out the Celtic. The new dialects were highly inflected and showed grammatical gender as did other Germanic languages. One of the dialects was to become the medium of the richest literature of Old English. This was the West Saxon of the time of King Alfred the Great at the end of the ninth century. For this reason West Saxon is the most easily and most often studied of old English dialects.

Christianity and the Latin of the church

In the latter part of the sixth century, Christianity made a religious conquest of England. It had made an earlier appearance toward the end of the Roman occupation, but this time it was adopted by the royal family and was to become a permanent part of English culture. Christian churchmen brought with them the scholarship so closely associated with the medieval church. Many Latin words, especially religious and scholastic terms, were borrowed by the English, and schools—always a stabilizing influence on language—were established.

Scandinavian invasion

In the eighth and ninth centuries, Norwegian and Danish Vikings raided the northern and eastern coast of England and the Danes almost succeeded in conquering all of England. For a brief time the English were subject to a Danish King, Canute. The Danes began to come as settlers as well as raiders and were, over several generations, assimilated into the population of the north-central part of England. They were culturally similar in many ways to the descendants of the Germanic tribes who had arrived 500 years before. Their language, too, was assimilated into the already established dialects of Old English. Many words in Modern English can be traced to a Danish origin but so easily were the languages combined that it is difficult, if not impossible, to compile definitive lists of words that were borrowed in contrast to native ones.

NOTES ON OLD ENGLISH AS A LANGUAGE

Since Old English scholars did not go in for extensive grammatical analysis of their language and compiled no dictionaries—as we know them—of the words they used, all we know of the structure of the language during that time must be based on a few scattered comments about the language contained in other works and an analysis of written records, Old English literature, and translations of works from other languages, primarily Latin.

The language began as a collection of dialects and since the Angles, Saxons, and Jutes settled different portions of the island, these dialect differences continued and, in some respects, became even more distinct after a time.

Within each dialect there were differences from one area to another and from one writer to another. Some can be attributed to geographic and social differences; some are built into the kinds of records that we have. Copies of various pieces of literature and other records were laboriously written out by hand. Scribes varied greatly in the amount, type and caliber of their education; each dealt with the language from the standpoint of his own dialect; and each had his own idiosyncrasies. Some were more faithful to that which they copied than others. Some helpfully added a great many notes in the margins; others very few. No one had taken on the responsibility of deciding upon a standard dialect, let alone what forms and structures within that dialect were preferred. Every scribe was his own guide to spelling, usage, and structure. Differences occur from one copyist to another and within the work of individuals; sometimes the same word is spelled several different ways on a single page.

While there were four major dialect areas and several minor ones, most of the scholarly research into the structure of Old English has been concentrated on the dialect of the West Saxon area—the south-westernmost part of the island—during the latter part of the ninth century.

Alfred the Great, who ruled the West Saxons from A.D. 871–899, was a good king in many ways, not the least of which was his encouragement of education and his respect for the literature, history and language of his people. Modern English developed from another of the early dialects, but, as a result of Alfred's encouragement and his own efforts as a translator, the richest collection of Old English writings is in the language of the West Saxons. The study of this dialect is therefore not only more fruitful in terms of language research but it also provides the key to reading and analysis of most of the literature of England up to the time of the Norman Conquest. The dialect we shall deal with here is that of the West Saxons. The reader should keep in mind that other varieties of the language did exist.

Old English was different in many ways from Modern English. Among these were differences in (1) the writing system, (2) the pronunciation or sound system, (3) the vocabulary, (4) the forms taken by various parts of speech, and (5) the syntax—or larger grammatical patterns. These differences are in many ways interdependent, but for purposes of clarity it is perhaps best to consider them one by one. As a basis for this consideration, it may be well to have a small sample of Old English to refer to. The interlinear translation is a purposely crude one consisting of word for word equivalents or near-equivalents in Modern English.

Fæder ure þu þe eart on heofonum, si þin nama gehalgod
Father our you that are in heaven   be your name hallowed
to-becume þin rice gewurþe þin willa on eorðan swa swa
come   thy kingdom become your will on earth so   so
on heofonum urne gedæghwamlican hlaf syle us to dæg
in heaven   our   daily   bread give us today
and forgyf us ure gyltas swa swa we forgyfa urum gyltendum
and forgive us our debts so so we forgive our   debtors
and ne gelæd þu us on costnunge ac alys us of yfele soþlice
and not lead you us in temptation but release us from evil truly

The writing system

The most striking difference between the passage above and a Modern English version of the Lord's prayer is the unfamiliar symbols or letters. The early Germanic peoples had made use of a set of symbols called the Runic Alphabet. But when adapting themselves to the teaching of Latin-oriented churchmen, they used Roman symbols except where there were sounds in Old English that had no equivalents in Latin. The strange symbols in the passage above are the *eth,* ð: *thorn,* þ; and *ashe,* æ. The ð and þ were used for the *th* sounds of Old

English, and the *æ* represented a vowel sound similar to the vowel in the Modern English word *cat*.

Pronunciation

The pronunciation of a speaker of Old English reading the prayer above would sound even more strange to modern ears than the written version looks to modern eyes.

The consonants of Old English would be similar to those of Modern English in many ways but there would be differences. Among these would be:

1. The *l* and *r* sounds would be more clearly defined.

2. The *h* that is little more than a breath in Modern English would be a tighter, more distinct sound in Old English—a close approximation is the sound represented by the *ch* in the Scottish word *loch*.

3. Some of the sounds that signal differences in Modern English were more nearly the same in Old English. For example, there seems to be no clearcut difference between the sounds symbolized by the ð and þ, just as there seem to be no clearly defined areas where the *f* and *v* sounds worked in contrast to each other as they do in such Modern English pairs as *five/fife* and *vat/fat*. In Old English the use of *f* and *v* sounds apparently were a matter of where the sounds occurred in relation to other sounds rather than a matter of signaling different meanings. Note the words *forgyf* and *yfele* in the prayer.

The vowels of Old English would probably sound more like those of modern European languages than like Modern English vowels.

1. Distinctions between long and short vowels would be a matter of duration alone. For example, the vowel sounds in the word *nama* are both similar to the *a* in the Modern English word *father,* but the first would be held for a longer time. The vowel in the Modern English word *name* is quite different in that it is a diphthong—a combination of one vowel sound sliding into another.

2. Diphthongs, or combinations of vowel sounds, did occur in Old English as in the word *heofonum,* but they were more distinctly two sounds than are the diphthongs of Modern English.

3. A vowel sound similar to the Modern French *u* was a part of the Old English vowel system. It was usually represented by the *y* symbol as in the word *yfele* in the prayer.

This vowel sound changed before English spelling was more or less firmly established but the consonant *ch* sound represented variously by the *h, gh* and *ch* of some English spellings remained into the late Middle English period and is therefore frozen into the spelling of words like *night, though,* and *cough.* This historical note is perhaps small comfort to the young student wrestling with his weekly spelling list, but it does demonstrate that such spellings are something more than mere perversity on the part of his elders.

Vocabulary

The vocabulary of Old English was still almost completely that of its Germanic heritage. The great bulk of Latin and French borrowings that are so frequent in Modern English had not yet come into the language. The number of words in the language was considerably smaller than the number in Modern English, but the elements of Old English were capable of expressing greatly varied and subtle meanings in the hands of imaginative writers. Speakers of Old English, and more particularly writers of the language, created new words when they needed them—as for example, when translating the more abstruse works of Latin—by combining elements of their native language. Modern English speakers do similar linguistic welding. Operating on the model of a term like *salesmanship,* they combine other forms for terms like *marksmanship, gamesmanship* and even *oneupmanship.* Such manipulation of the language is often regarded with haughty disdain by some modern purists but Old English writers were far more flexible in this regard and, while they adopted many words from their Latin sources, they were even more likely to attempt to say the same thing with their own resources. One example is in the prayer. The term *gedæghwamlican* is made up of the forms *dæg* (day), *hwam* (anything) and the prefix-suffix combination *ge- -lice* (alike). The *-an* is an inflectional suffix. These have simply been molded together to express the notion "any—or all—days alike" and, therefore, *daily.*

Parts of speech and inflection

We have said that Old English was a highly inflected language. This is the next most striking difference between Old English and

Modern English. Nouns, pronouns, adjectives, verbs, and adverbs had complex systems of endings or vowel changes or both. These systems can only be suggested here for reasons of space, but a look at even a few representative examples will demonstrate the extent to which Old English differs in this respect from the language that we use today.

Nouns and adjectives

The nouns and adjectives of Old English were adapted to various uses in phrases and sentences by means of inflectional suffixes or endings added to the root or stem form. They were different in two important ways from the highly simplified inflections of Modern English—the plural and possessive inflections added to nouns and the *-er* and *-est* added to simple adjectives to produce the comparative and superlative degree.

First, nouns and adjectives showed *grammatical gender*. In learning the language—as when learning modern European languages—the grammatical gender of each noun must be learned along with its referential meaning. These are purely arbitrary and have no relation to natural gender. For example, the words *sunne* (sun) and *heorte* (heart) are feminine; the words *steorra* (star) and *wyfmann* (woman) are masculine; and *cild* (child) is neuter, regardless of the sex of the young person in question. Adjectives had forms adapting them to use with each gender-type of noun.

Second, nouns were adapted by inflectional ending for use as subjects, direct objects, and indirect objects in addition to the possessive form which still exists in English. These are the *cases* referred to by grammarians as Nominative, Accusative, Dative, and Genitive. A second set of endings adapted the noun stems for use as plurals in each of the four cases.

Adjectives not only had to match the gender of the nouns they modified but the case and number as well. In addition, another complete set of inflections for adjectives made their appearance when the adjective was preceded by a definite article, a possessive or demonstrative pronoun. These latter forms were also subject to extensive inflection. Some forms still existed for yet another case, the Instrumental, which served to indicate the means by which an action was performed. Sets of inflectional endings varied depending on the sound makeup of the stem form of nouns and some adjectives, but the representative sets below will serve to illustrate the kinds of inflections that appear in Old English.

REPRESENTATIVE ENDINGS FOR MASCULINE, FEMININE AND NEUTER NOUNS IN OLD ENGLISH

		Masculine	Feminine	Neuter
Singular	Nominative	—	-u	—
	Genitive	-es	-e	-es
	Accusative	—	-e	—
	Dative/Instr.	-e	-e	-e
Plural	Nominative	-as	-a	—
	Genitive	-a	-a	-a
	Accusative	-as	-a	—
	Dative/Instr.	-um	-um	-um

INFLECTIONAL ENDINGS ADDED TO ADJECTIVES IN OLD ENGLISH
STRONG DECLENSION

(For use when adjective alone modified the noun)

		Masculine	Feminine	Neuter
Singular	Nominative	—	—	—
	Genitive	-es	-re	-es
	Accusative	-ne	-e	—
	Dative	-um	-re	-um
	Instrumental	-e	-re	-e
Plural	Nominative	-e	-a	—
	Genitive	-ra	-ra	-ra
	Accusative	-e	-a	—
	Dative/Instr.	-um	-um	-um

WEAK DECLENSION

(For use when the adjective was preceded by a definite article, a demonstrative or a possessive pronoun)

		Masculine	Feminine	Neuter
Singular	Nominative	-a	-e	-e
	Genitive	-an	-an	-an
	Accusative	-an	-an	-an
	Dative/Instr.	-an	-an	-an
Plural	Nominative	—	-an	—
	Genitive	—	-ra	—
	Accusative	—	-an	—
	Dative/Instr.	—	-um	—

To illustrate the uses of these forms in combination it is necessary to list the declension—or set of forms—taken by the definite article in Old English. An interesting fact about these forms is that they served as both the definite article and the demonstrative pronoun *that*.

DECLENSION OF THE DEFINITE ARTICLE IN OLD ENGLISH

| | *Singular* | | | *Plural* |
	Masculine	*Feminine*	*Neuter*	*All Genders*
Nominative	sē	sēo	þæt	þā
Genitive	þæs	þǣre	þæs	þāra
Accusative	þone	þā	þæt	þā
Dative	þǣm	þǣre	þǣm	þǣm
Instrumental	þȳ	þǣre	þȳ	þǣm

Lines above the vowels indicate that they are long rather than short. Again, the distinction is one of duration only, not a change in the shape of the vowel.

Adding the noun inflections to a masculine noun, *hām* (home), a feminine noun, *stōw* (place), and a neuter noun, *hūs* (house), and the adjective endings to a single adjective, *gōd* (good), we can see how the resulting forms work both with and without a definite article.

The differences in Modern English inflection are more apparent in writing than in actual speech. The speech sounds of Modern English produce only two forms, *home* and *homes,* but we consider that we have both a plural and a possessive form plus a combination of the two. The only real complexity that we add is the *-er* and *-est* inflection that we add to adjectives to produce the comparative and superlative degrees. The comparative and superlative degrees of our adjective *good* are slightly different but we still may speak of *good homes, better homes,* and *best homes.* These differences, however, also existed in Old English so that in order to see the full range of adjective inflection working in Old English we would find it necessary to multiply the forms in the following charts by three!

It is well to keep in mind that while we may be confused—or even horrified—by this necessity for speakers of Old English to learn large sets of inflections in order to use their nouns and adjectives, they would be likely to find it just as confusing to master the rules of word order by which we make some of the same distinctions. We have grown up with our word order; they grew up with their inflections. Even so, they too must have found so many inflections a problem because the weakening of inflectional distinctions had begun even in Old English times.

STRONG ADJECTIVES

		Adj.	Masc. Noun	Modern Forms
Singular	Nom.	gōd	hām	good homes
	Gen.	gōdes	hāmes	good home's
	Acc.	gōdne	hām	good home
	Dative	gōdum	hāme	good home
	Instr.	gōde	hāme	good home
Plural	Nom.	gōde	hāmas	good homes
	Gen.	gōdra	hāma	good homes'
	Acc.	gōde	hāmas	good homes
	D/Instr.	gōdum	hāmum	good homes

			Fem. Noun	
Singular	Nom.	gōd	stōw	good place
	Gen.	gōdre	stōwe	good place's
	Acc.	gōde	stōwe	good place
	D/Instr.	gōdum	stōwum	good place
Plural	Nom.	gōda	stōwa	good places
	Gen.	gōdra	stōwa	good places'
	Acc.	gōda	stōwa	good places
	D/Instr.	gōdum	stōwum	good places

			Neut. Noun	
Singular	Nom.	gōd	hūs	good house
	Gen.	gōdes	hūses	good house's
	Acc.	gōd	hūs	good house
	Dative	gōdum	hūse	good house
	Instr.	gōde	hūse	good house
Plural	Nom.	gōd	hūs	good houses
	Gen.	gōdra	hūsa	good houses'
	Acc.	gōd	hūs	good houses
	D/Instr.	gōdum	hūsum	good houses

This weakening is obvious from the charts above which show that, at the stage of development represented by these forms, many inflections were similar or had already fallen together.

Pronouns

The pronouns of Modern English retain more inflectional adaptations than any other group of words in the language. It is, therefore, perhaps easier to consider Old English inflection in terms of these forms in each period than to attempt to compare differences in noun and adjective forms from each period.

WEAK ADJECTIVES

Def. Art.	Adj.	Masc. Noun	Modern Forms
sē	gōda	hām	the good home
þæs	gōdan	hāmes	the good home's
þone	gōdan	hām	the good home
þǣm	gōdan	hāme	the good home
þȳ	gōdan	hāme	the good home
þā	gōdan	hāmas	the good homes
þāra	gōdra	hāma	the good homes
þā	gōdan	hāmas	the good homes
þǣm	gōdum	hāmum	the good homes

		Fem. Noun	
sēo	gōde	stōw	the good place
þǣre	gōdan	stōwe	the good place's
þā	gōdan	stōwe	the good place
þǣm	gōdan	stōwe	the good place
þā	gōdan	stōwa	the good places
þāra	gōdan	stōwa	the good places'
þā	gōdan	stōwa	the good places
þǣm	gōdum	stōwum	the good places

		Neut. Noun	
þæt	gōde	hūs	the good house
þæs	gōdan	hūses	the good house's
þæt	gōde	hūs	the good house
þǣm	gōdan	hūse	the good house
þȳ	gōdan	hūse	the good house
þā	gōdan	hūs	the good houses
þāra	gōdra	hūsa	the good houses'
þā	gōdan	hūsa	the good houses
þǣm	gōdum	hūsum	the good houses

In the following chart, forms that are still to be found in Modern English have been included in parentheses. Other Old English forms have disappeared completely or have fallen together with similar forms.

It is apparent that the second person singular forms ðū, ðīn, and ðē became *thou, thine* and *thee* and later gave way to the second person plural forms *you* and *your*. A second interesting point concerns the dual number which has been lost completely. The distinctions made with these forms must now be made by such constructions as "we two" and "the two of us."

Demonstrative pronouns total four in Modern English—*this, these, that,* and *those*—as compared to about forty forms in Old English. The interrogative pronouns show a similar depletion of forms.

DECLENSION OF PERSONAL PRONOUNS IN OLD ENGLISH

		First Person		Second Person		Third Person			
Singular	Nom.	ic	(I)	ðū	(you)	hē	(he)	hēo (she)	hit (it)
	Gen.	mīn	(mine)	ðīn	(your)	his	(his)	hiere (her)	his (its)
	Acc.	mec, mē	(me)	ðec, ðē	(you)	hine (him)	hīe	(her)	hit (it)
	Dative	mē		ðē		him	hiere		him
Dual	Nom.	wit		git					
	Gen.	uncer		incer					
	Acc/Dat.	unc		inc					
Plural	Nom.	wē	(we)	gē	(you)		hīe	(they)	
	Gen.	ūre, ūser	(our)	ēower	(your)		hiera	(their)	
	Acc.	ūsic, ūs	(us)	ēowic,ēow	(you)		hīe	(them)	
	Dative	ūs		ēow			him		

Verbs

The verbs of Old English fall into two major types, *weak verbs* and *strong verbs*. Verbs in the *weak* category had past and participle forms made by adding "dental suffixes" to the stem form. (Dental suffixes include a *d, t,* or *th* sound, all of which are made by placing the tip of the tongue behind the upper front teeth, hence the name.) There are three minor categories with some variation in the pattern of changes. But the important point about weak verbs is that these changes became, by analogy, the regular means of adapting new verbs to syntactic function in English. Many of the strong verbs were later adapted to the pattern so that the overwhelming majority of verbs in Modern English follow similar patterns and we now speak of verbs like *talk/talked, work/worked, row/rowed* as the *regular verbs* in English.

Strong verbs, which are the linguistic ancestors of Modern English *irregular verbs* such as *ring/rang/rung, drive/drove/driven,* and *speak/spoke/spoken,* had past and participle forms that involved changing the vowel in the root verb. The members of each class had a distinctive pattern of forms depending on consideration of such matters as the vowel in the root form, the consonant sounds following the vowel, whether the root was a single syllable or two, and the vowel of the second syllable when there was one. Complex factors of sound and combinations of sound must be studied to understand the workings of the seven classes of strong verbs. There were over 300 strong verbs in Old English. Some have been supplanted by borrowed verbs, a great many others have joined the regular verbs so that there are less than half that many irregular verbs in Modern English.

Both strong and weak verbs in Old English were inflected to show person (first, second, and third); number (singular and plural); tense (past and present); and mood (indicative, subjunctive, and im-

perative). All of these inflections took the form of suffixes except for
the prefix *ge-* added to form the past participle of most of the weak
verbs and some of the strong ones. Simple multiplication shows that
each verb had two dozen or more forms as opposed to the three to five
forms of Modern English verbs. The verb *eat* has five forms in Modern
English, *eat/eats/ate/eaten/eating;* the verb *hit* has only three, *hit/
hits/hitting.*

Syntax

All of this tagging parts of speech with their function in phrases
and sentences meant that word order in these larger structures could
be much more varied than that allowed by simpler Modern English
forms. For example, look at an Old English sentence such as

Þa het se cyning hie sittan, and hie swa dydon; and hie sona
Then commanded the king them sit and they so did and they soon
him lifes word ætgædere mid eallum his geferum þe þær æt
him life's word together with all his companions that there at
wæron bodedon and lærdon.
were preached and taught.

This sentence must be reordered something like "Then the king commanded them to sit down and they sat and preached and taught life's
word to him and to all of his companions who were there," in order for
it to be easily understood by a reader of Modern English.

Prepositions and other words used to establish syntactic relationships in Modern English carried a far lighter linguistic burden in Old
English. Prepositions could occur following the noun they worked with
or even be separated from it by another word or phrase. The inflectional
labels were on hand to sort out the relationships. But the labels became
blurred and less and less distinct over the years, and relationships they
had established were made more and more often by other means.

THE MIDDLE ENGLISH PERIOD 1066–1500

During the years of Scandinavian expansion in the eighth and
ninth centuries when bands of Danes raided and settled in England,
other Norsemen had found the northeastern coastlands of France more
to their liking. The Norman French were descendants of these Norsemen

who had become absorbed into the French population. Their language was a dialect of Old French.

In January 1066, the English throne was vacated by the death of a childless king, Edward the Confessor. William, Duke of Normandy, was Edward's second cousin and considered himself rightful heir to the throne. Since the English nobles disagreed, William invaded the island, confiscated the lands of the English and granted them to the French who had supported him.

England now became a land of three languages. Norman French was the language of the court, of government and the new upper social classes; Latin was still the language of the Church; English was still spoken by the masses of English people, forced now into the status of lower classes.

The English nobles had been almost completely wiped out in the bloody conquest and the rebellious uprisings that followed. By the end of the eleventh century virtually all of those who held political or social power and many of those in powerful Church positions were of Norman French origin. Important written records of the time, with the single exception of the Anglo-Saxon Chronicle, which was continued through 1154, are in French. Those in power spoke French; those who were literate read and wrote French; those who could educate their children educated them in French; and any young man who sought to earn his keep as a scribe learned Latin and French because there was no market for such services in English.

The realm made up of England and the Dukedom of Normandy began to show signs of cracking apart as early as the reign of Henry III, 1216–1272. By then the Anglo-Norman nobles were, as often as not, of mixed Norman-English descent but of English birth. Their resentment of domination by their mainland brothers grew and their sense of English identity asserted itself. Many were bilingual and, since the French and English languages had existed side by side for over a century, the two now had a sizeable area of common vocabulary.

The Hundred Years' War, from the middle of the fourteenth century to the middle of the fifteenth, at last brought about the complete separation of the two nations. The nobility in England still spoke French but bit by bit English came back into the schools, the law courts and government, and regained social status. It made the final step back to a position of importance when it emerged once again as a respected literary medium with the Wycliff translation of the Bible and the writing of Chaucer, Langland, and others in the fourteenth century.

It was not the same English that had bowed to Norman French. Not only had the grammatical pattern of the language altered considerably, but the vocabulary, too, had greatly changed. A tremendous number of French words had entered the language in every area of life. Speakers of English had freely adopted nouns, verbs, and adjectives from the French and since most had become good, serviceable linguistic material, they were now a part of the English language. English was vastly richer in vocabulary and, in addition, a custom had been established. Englishmen continued to be avid word-borrowers. England was never again to be invaded; no other language was to be forced upon Englishmen. But when England herself engaged in political and economic expansion, her people were to gather useful words from every corner of the world. They not only borrowed words but made use of parts of other languages—notably Greek and Latin—when coining new words such as all those that begin with *tele-* and all those that end with *-ology*. The word *linguistic* is, itself, built upon the Latin word *lingua* or tongue.

Over the years of the Middle English period, class distinctions based on whether one spoke French or English gave way to class distinctions based upon which dialect of English was spoken. As in most countries, the prestige dialect became that of the political, social, and economic center of the country. In England, the East Midland dialect —that of London—emerged as Standard English.

NOTES ON MIDDLE ENGLISH AS A LANGUAGE

The period from 1066 to about 1500 was one of great change for those who spoke the dialects of what is now called Middle English.

The single most significant fact of the early part of this period as far as the development of the English language is concerned was the steady erosion of the Old English inflectional systems. The dialects of Old English had already shown tendencies toward dropping a great many of their inflections; conditions following the Norman Conquest were ideal for speeding up this process. English existed for a century and a half almost entirely as a spoken language with the restraints of scholarship, literature, and social pressure lifted. Whole sets of inflections weakened, became less distinct and some finally dropped completely from the language.

The single most important fact of the later years of the Middle English period as far as the development of the language was concerned was the emergence of the London dialect as Standard English. This dialect, along with all the others, was steadily changing. Choosing a single stage of the development of a single dialect as representative of the entire period will be based at least in part on literary merit. The notes here will be on the dialect of London during the latter part of the fourteenth century and, more specifically, on the language used by the poet Geoffrey Chaucer. Again it is well to keep in mind the fact that other dialects did exist and some even influenced the development of the standard dialect. For purposes of a very general comparison of Middle English with Modern English, here is part of the description of one of the Canterbury pilgrims from the Prologue to *The Canterbury Tales:*

A clerk ther was of Oxenford also,
That un-to logik hadde longe y-go.   (y-go = gone)
As lene was his hors as is a rake
And he nas not right fat, I undertake;
But loked holwe, and ther-to soberly . . .   (holwe = hol-
                                                    low)

But al be that he was a philosophre,
Yet hadde he but litel gold in cofre,
But al that he might-e of his freendes hente,   (hente =
                                                    received)

On bokes and on lerninge he it spente,
And bisily gan for the soules preye
Of hem that yaf him wher-with to scoleye.   (scoleye =
                                                    study)

Of studie took he most cure and most hede.   (cure = care)
Nought o word spak he more than was nede,
And that was seyd in forme and reverence,
And short and quik and ful of hy sentence.   (sentence =
                                                    meaning)

Souninge in moral vertu was his speche,   (souninge =
                                                    resounding)

And gladly wolde he lerne, and gladly teche.

It is not necessary to translate the lines above beyond pointing out the few words that have dropped from the language and those that have a somewhat different meaning in Modern English. If nothing else the passage above shows how much more the language of Chaucer was like present day English than Anglo-Saxon was. But differences did exist in (1) pronunciation, (2) vocabulary, (3) inflection, and (4) syntax. As with Old English, or any other language for that matter, these linguistic areas are interdependent, but we will probably avoid confusion by considering them one by one.

Pronunciation

Scribes of Chaucer's time had one advantage over writers of Modern English. They were not so rigidly bound by historical precedent in matters of spelling. For the most part they spelled words as they said them, and we can gather much information about how the language sounded by carefully studying the written forms.

It can safely be assumed that the consonants that appear in Middle English spelling were not silent. Some borrowed terms, such as the word *philosophre* in the passage above brought foreign spelling conventions with them, but others were changed to match their English pronunciation.

Among the striking differences between the consonant pronunciations of a fourteenth-century Londoner and the consonant sounds of Modern English are

1. the more distinct pronunciation of sounds represented by the *l* in *wolde* and the *r* in *leringe* in the passage above.

2. the sound, like the final sound in *loch,* represented by the *gh* in *nought* and *might-e* above.

3. initial consonant combinations like the *kn* of *knight* and the *gn* of *gnarled* were pronounced as spelled. Speakers of Modern English still begin words with consonant combinations like *kl/gl* and *kr/gr,* but we have dispensed with the *kn/gn* combinations in initial position in our speech if not in our spelling.

The vowels of Middle English still had their "continental" values. Generally speaking, the following symbols represented sounds similar to those in the Modern English examples:

> **a** for the vowel sound in Modern English *father*
> **e** for the vowel sound in Modern English *they* or *preyed*
> **i** for the vowel sound in Modern English *sit*
> **y** for the vowel sound in Modern English *priest*
> **ou, ow** for the vowel sound in Modern English *rule*
> **o** for the vowel sound in Modern English *hole*
> **oo** for the vowel sound in Modern English *fought*

Some vowel sounds were longer than others. "Long" and "short" still refer to duration in Middle English vowel sounds, but the long vowels had apparently already begun to take on more of a tense quality (produced physically by the shape of the lips) than their short counter-parts.

Pronunciation of still another important sound, represented by the final *e* in such words as the *nede, speche,* and *teche* in the passage above will be considered in the note below on inflection.

Vocabulary

During the years of the Middle English period, literally thousands of French words were adopted into the English language. In some in-stances these replaced Old English terms; more often they were adopted to use as similar but not identical terms as in the case of *mansion, plume,* and *beef* which settled in easily beside *house, feather,* and *cow.* It is not surprising that the words borrowed from a language associated with the nobility often came to have more elegant connotations than the native English words.

Borrowing on a large scale did not begin immediately with the coming of the French. Speakers of the two languages continued to live and work together with the two languages remaining separate for the most part. Later, when greater numbers of people of the ruling class became bilingual, the language barrier broke and French words flooded into the English vocabulary. A quick check of the etymological nota-tions on any page of a Modern English dictionary will give ample evidence of the extent of this borrowing.

Many thousands of French nouns, adjectives, and verbs became a part of English during this period, including such basic terms as *blue, faith, music,* and *art.* The words *government, court, religion, fashion, dinner, medicine,* and *military* are all of French origin; and each could head a list of dozens or even hundreds of words that came from French into English, giving the language a distinctly Latinate flavor. Still it is important to realize that the core of the language remained English. English speakers kept their articles, pronouns, prepositions, and words for the most fundamental parts of the language—numbers, body parts, family relationships, and words like *day, night, fire, water, God, earth, stone, tree, life, death, eat, drink,* and *sleep.* English borrowed freely, but English it remained.

Inflection

Germanic pronunciation places strong stress on the root or stem of inflected words. Sounds in these stressed syllables, and particularly the vowel sounds, tend to be more distinct than those in unstressed or lightly stressed syllables. Sounds in the lightly stressed inflections in Old English began to lose their distinct qualities even before the period of the Norman Conquest. The first few centuries of what is now called the Middle English period saw this tendency develop into a full-fledged shift in the nature of the English language.

The progressive loss of distinct inflections began with the shift of final -*m* to -*n* in some noun and adjective endings. The vowel sounds in these inflections lost their distinct qualities and fell together in most cases to a sound still common in the unstressed syllables of many words in Modern English. The italicized, unstressed vowels in *a*bout, *e*lect, and c*a*reer show this pronunciation. Modern phonology assigns the symbol [ə] to this vowel sound. Further erosion of the inflections involved loss of the final -*n* so that many inflections that had once shown a variety of forms now shared a simple [ə] sound. Later, even the final [ə] became less and less distinct and finally disappeared altogether.

In written language, the final -*e* was still a phonetic spelling. Therefore, where a final -*e* does occur, it must be pronounced in reading the poetry so that the rhyme scheme is not distorted. For example, both *lene* and *rake* are two syllable words in the line "As lene was his hors as is a rake." You can demonstrate the difference this makes by reading the line aloud, pronouncing *lene* and *rake* as single syllables and then reading it again giving each form the two syllables that Chaucer intended.

Englishmen spoke the inflections of the language in a variety of ways during the middle English period. Slowly, steadily, the inflections gave way until, by the end of the period, all adjective inflections for gender, person, number, and case were virtually dead.

A few noun inflections remained strong and even absorbed other forms. Among these were the -*s* and -*es* endings that showed plural number and the genitive or possessive case. Other plurals, such as the -*en* form most prevalent in the southern dialect, finally fell to the -*s* endings except in a few forms such as *children* and *oxen*.

Pronouns, because of their different syntactic function and because they depend far less on unaccented final symbols for their different forms, were slower to change. Even though a great many of these forms became unnecessary as other means of making grammatical distinctions became more common, they retain more inflection than any other part of speech in Modern English.

Two important changes mark the verbs of Middle English. First, verb inflections leveled along with the general trend throughout the language. Second, many of the strong verbs of Old English came to follow the patterns of the more numerous weak verbs in taking past and participle forms. The strong, or irregular verbs, that remain in

Modern English are among the most troublesome forms for both foreign speakers and children to learn for two reasons. First, they are far fewer in number. Second, the shifts in the pronunciation of vowels by speakers of the language have obscured the once-regular patterns of change from present to past to participle forms for each class.

Grammatical gender in any language is largely supported by the differences in inflectional forms in the language. A natural consequence of the loss of inflection is, then, the loss of these distinctions of grammatical gender. Pronouns, on the other hand, have a stronger tendency to recognize natural gender, and the pronouns of English are probably the basis for the gradual shift toward recognition of natural gender that we have in Modern English.

Syntax

As inflection fell from power in English, the syntactic distinctions once made by these forms were more and more often made by placing words in relation to each other in phrases and sentences in ways that indicated their function, such as which nouns served as subject and object and which adjectives worked with which nouns.

Prepositions, conjunctions, relative pronouns, and other such forms were given more responsibility as linguistic signals. These changes, like the inflectional changes, came about slowly. Word order and the workings of prepositions, conjunctions, and other such forms were by no means clearly defined at any point during Middle English times. Phrase and sentence structure were still largely a matter of personal preference, but certain conventions were becoming more and more like those of Modern English. Even if some of the constructions in Chaucer's description of the Clerk appear odd to modern eyes, there are enough recognizable signals to allow fairly easy understanding of the passage by a modern reader.

THE MODERN ENGLISH PERIOD 1500–THE PRESENT

The Renaissance came late to England, but it arrived compounded by several factors that had a profound effect upon the English language. Among these were the introduction of the printing press into England, the spread of education to greater numbers of people outside the ruling class, and greater trade and communication both among the people of England and between the English and the peoples of the other countries of Europe and the world.

Printing and widespread education served to enforce a standard dialect; more rapid communication and exchange of ideas stimulated both the enlargement of the vocabulary of English and the spread of English to other countries.

Latin and Greek were recognized as the languages of the Western world's great literary heritage and of great scholarship, but translators were rapidly making great literary works available in English. Translators and scholars borrowed heavily from the Latin vocabulary of their source materials during this period and enormous numbers of Latin words became English words. These, added to the vocabulary already borrowed from the French and those added during earlier periods of borrowing from Latin, contributed to the decidedly Latinate flavor of Modern English.

English spelling had always been largely a matter of personal preference. Now the rapidly expanding use of printing and the needs of the schools began to set standard spellings for most words. These were established to a great extent before the last important shift in the language occurred.

The great vowel shift

This important change, called the Great Vowel Shift, involved changes in the pronunciation of the long vowels in English. These changes, like those of the Germanic Consonant Shift, were highly systematic and very gradual.

These changes in pronunciation resulted when the positioning of the jaw and tongue was raised slightly for each of the long vowels. For example, the back vowel [o] occurred in the word *tooth*. The word was pronounced in Middle English times to rhyme with the Modern English pronunciation of *both,* but gradually shifted to its present pronunciation rhyming with *booth*. Front long vowels underwent similar changes. The word *me*—pronounced in Middle English times to rhyme with the present pronunciation of *they*—moved up to its present pronunciation. The highest long vowels—the [i] in front and the [u] in back—became combinations or diphthongs. The Great Vowel Shift can be charted, very loosely, this way:

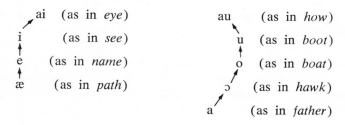

Examples of the sounds are found in the Modern English words in parentheses. To arrive at Middle English pronunciations, we must substitute the pronunciation of the next lower vowel—their position before the shift. In some words the vowel sounds were affected by the consonant or vowel sounds immediately preceding or following them.

The Great Vowel Shift took place very gradually beginning about 1500 and was almost complete by about 1750. It is largely because of this shifting pronunciation that present English spellings of many words—more or less fixed before the shift—is not consistent with modern pronunciations.

Other modern developments

In the eighteenth century, attempts were made to fix grammatical rules for English. As noted in the section on language study, those who sought to establish some orderly description of the grammar of English were often too intent upon making English grammar conform to the grammatical system of Latin. Their rules had an effect on the English language and its use. For example, many students are still taught that English verbs have a past, present and future tense. In the words of Professor Albert Baugh, ". . . it could no longer be said that English was a language without rules. It might almost be said that we had too many rules."

The English language spread with the British Empire, was adapted to new uses, and adapted itself to others. Many now feel that it is the nearest thing possible to a world language. It is the native tongue of a large portion of the world's population, and it is the second language of still another great number. It may never become a universal language, but it is already highly negotiable international linguistic currency.

Obviously the English language has not stopped growing and changing. As more modern methods have been applied to the study of the language, there has been a tendency to recognize dialect differences and varieties of usage for what they are rather than attempting to pin "right" and "wrong" labels to them. Socially approved Standard British English and Standard American English dialects are recognized but even these are subject to change under the pressure of changing usage.

Many important details have been omitted here, but even this brief summary of the history of our language gives some indication of the tremendous complexity of the forces that formed the language that modern grammar methods seek to describe.

The structure of Modern English has been described in many ways. The language is enormously complex, flexible, and creative. It is not surprising that there are many ways to approach a description of how it works. Most of those engaged in the grammatical analysis of English are willing to admit that problems arise no matter which approach is followed. Those who write school textbooks have found that each approach has merit, and many use whatever appears to be most useful from each of the major approaches to the problem of describing English grammar.

These major approaches, the traditional, structural, and generative, are quite different in some respects, quite similar in others. Any evaluation of work that borrows freely from all three must be based on some knowledge of each method on its own terms. For this reason it is best to consider the methods and results of traditional, structural, and generative grammarians separately.

4

TRADITIONAL GRAMMAR IN THE SCHOOLS

One problem that besets linguistic researcher and language teacher alike is the decision as to where to begin an analysis of the grammar of a language. The simplest sentence in any language involves the sound system of the language, the combinations of sound that carry bits of meaning, the meanings attached to the combinations, and the more involved or complex arrangements of the meaning units. Some agenda for dealing with all these aspects of the language must be decided upon. It is a task similar to that of assigning seniority to the chicken or the egg—except that all the aspects of the language process make their appearance simultaneously.

Long ago the Greeks began by sorting the words of their language according to their meaning. They worked from there to combinations of words and, later, took up the study of units used to make up words. One consequence of choosing words as a starting point was that their study of language was well along and emphasis had already been placed on the written forms of Greek before consideration was given to the smallest language units. Thus, "smallest units" was assumed to mean letters rather than the sounds that the letters represented. Another consequence of beginning with words and defining them according to meaning, regardless of the language in question, is the necessity for definitions that do not allow for the adaptability of many English words. If, for example, nouns are the names of things and verbs are the names of actions, what—precisely—is the difference between a thing and an action? Is *painting* a thing or an action? The definer is forced to put his words into larger contexts in order to explain that "things" are what we talk about. In "The children are painting," the children are being talked about; in "Painting is a pleasant pastime for children," the painting is being talked about. Clear enough, perhaps, but what has happened to the decision to begin by defining words and their meaning? We are already up to our knees in syntax.

Nevertheless, an absolutely necessary choice—beginning *somewhere*—was made and a tradition established. This tradition was reinforced and carried into schools and teaching by the firm conviction among scholars and teachers that it was the least of several possible evils. A student of grammar spoke and wrote words, they could be listed in isolation and discussed—however circuitously—as linguistic units. The choice has by no means been abandoned. Many still feel that grammars that begin with consideration of words and their meanings are more efficient than others both for analyzing a language and for teaching the grammar of a language. The question has been debated at great length and with great heat; it will not be resolved here.

The influence of any tradition is, in some measure, based on the very fact that it *is* traditional—or "has always been done that way." Any tradition is best understood in terms of the conditions at the time of its beginning. In order to understand the stronghold established by traditional grammar methods in the schools of England and America, some consideration must be given to goals and problems particular to teaching, and even more specifically, to the goals and problems of teachers of English in England in the fifteenth and sixteenth centuries. Among the goals of English teachers and school grammarians of the time were:

1. Establishing for English a position of dignity and respect among the languages of the Western World.

2. Establishing ground rules for the standard or prestige dialect which was the social goal of the parents of their students.

3. Devising methods of presenting the facts of English grammar that would be most efficient for both teacher and students.

4. Organizing the study of English grammar for English speaking students.

Among the problems of these teachers and grammarians were:

1. The fact that for centuries "grammar" had been synonymous with Latin grammar, the knowledge of which was the mark of the educated man.

2. Schools were becoming open to greater numbers of students from the lower and middle classes, with education serving as a means of upward social mobility. For the new masses of students, the study of English grammar was not so much an objective study of the communicative skills of man as it was a utilitarian mastery of the kind of language that would enable them to succeed educationally, socially, economically, and politically.

3.   Since Latin grammar was a part of the curriculum of English schools, the terminology and the methods of discussing Latin grammar were already understood and respected by teachers and were a part of every student's educational life.

4.   Teaching Latin was simply a matter of presenting established, unchanging rules of a "dead" language, that is, one not spoken by any people as their everyday medium of communication and, therefore, not subject to shifts in meaning and usage. Teaching English was a matter of presenting the rules for a language that the students themselves knew and used daily with a wide range of individual differences. A living, changing language is much harder to pin down, especially for native speakers who bring other convictions about that language and other language habits into the classroom with them.

Writers of school grammars and teachers relied on the commonly known Latin grammar for terminology and method, the prestige of recognized English writers and poets for criteria of usage and meaning, and the lever of social pressure for establishing themselves as arbiters of English grammar.

In several ways their choices were understandable ones for that time and that place. First, students could deal with both Latin and English using the same terminology and the word grammar plan of attack. How many modern students report that they "never understood English grammar until they studied Latin?" The disservice done to English grammar was in the unreasonable degree to which English was manipulated to reconcile the very real differences between the two languages.

Second, English school grammarians and teachers could plead innocent to the charge of creating a prestige dialect. Social, economic, and political factors had accomplished that much already. Certain usages were already recognized as socially acceptable or preferable to others. Putting these into text books had the effect of freezing them into this designation while, in some cases, custom and usage continued to change. Grammarians and teachers were culpable only as accessories after the fact, insisting on rigid rules of right and wrong, older preferences over newer ones, regardless of change even among well-educated speakers and writers.

Third, while simple, easily memorized notional definitions of parts of speech and grammatical constructions were often circular and uncertain and subject to great numbers of "exceptions," they were, nevertheless, a starting point, a place to begin the study of English grammar; and no one had proposed a more effective means of dealing with that very fundamental classroom problem.

Some changes have come about in school texts making use of traditional grammar methods over the years. Recognition of the importance of spoken forms of languages brought "phonics" to the teaching of reading and widened the area covered by the first two of the three R's to include the four language arts—reading, writing, speaking, and listening.

No modern school grammar insists that English must be equated with Latin grammar. Few insist on such usage as the subjunctive "If that be true," instead of "If that is true," or the future tense construction "I shall arrive by plane" instead of "I will arrive by plane." Most recognize that usage differs with situation and none would suggest, for example, that an informal note inviting a friend for dinner should be worded as a wedding invitation is worded.

Still, the traditional word-grammar analysis is the basis for describing the grammar of English in many school texts. Written language is still seen by many to be more carefully constructed and therefore more worth studying.

There is a great deal of variation among traditional grammars, especially in recent years, but the grammars that still retain their traditional framework generally follow the pattern of analysis and definitions listed below.

I. Parts of speech and accidence

The words of the English language may be divided into eight categories based on the ideas that they signify or the functions they perform in larger structures or both. The eight *parts of speech* are nouns, pronouns, adjectives, verbs, adverbs, prepositions, conjunctions, and interjections. Some of these parts of speech take a variety of forms depending on their syntactic use. These forms are referred to as *accidence*.

1. NOUNS   A noun is typically defined as the name of a person, place, or thing. A more detailed definition also includes the grammatical uses, or functions of these forms. Nouns appear as subjects, direct and indirect objects, predicate nominatives, appositives, and so on. Some words

that ordinarily appear as other parts of speech, such as *red* and *help,* and even whole clauses may also fulfill these functions as in "Red is a pretty color"; "His only wish was to help"; and "That he helped her was not surprising." Such usages are grouped together with nouns and pronouns under the cover term *substantive. Gerunds* are verb forms ending in *-ing* that are used as substantives. For example, "Swimming is fun." English nouns have a *common* and a *possessive* or *genitive case* and they show *singular* and *plural number.*

2. PRONOUNS A pronoun is defined as a word that substitutes for a noun. Subclasses of pronouns are sorted on the basis of types of nouns for which they substitute and on the basis of their grammatical uses or functions. Subclasses of pronouns include *personal pronouns, possessive pronouns, relative pronouns, interrogative pronouns, demonstrative pronouns, reflexive pronouns,* and *indefinite pronouns.*

There are comparatively few pronouns in the English language and the various categories are usually given a very brief definition and the forms listed. For example, the demonstratives are this/that/these/those; the relative pronouns are who/whom/which/that and so on. Personal pronouns have *nominative, objective,* and *possessive cases.* Personal pronouns, demonstratives, and reflexives show *singular* and *plural number.*

In some grammars possessive and demonstrative pronouns are also listed as adjectives when they are used as modifiers for nouns.

3. ADJECTIVES An adjective is defined as a word that modifies a noun or other substantive. In addition to the pronouns that double as adjectives, there are nouns that also modify other nouns and are said to be used as adjectives when they do so as in "state fair" and "sidewalk café."

Adjectives show *degree.* Examples of the *positive, comparative* and *superlative degrees* are long/longer/longest and pretty/prettier/prettiest. Some adjectives make use of *periphrastic comparison* as, for example, beautiful/more beautiful/most beautiful.

Adjectives usually appear immediately preceding the noun they modify or as predicate adjectives following the *copula* or *linking verbs,* as in "John is tall" or "Mary seems happy."

4. VERBS A verb is a word that expresses action or a state of being. Traditional grammar recognizes three kinds of English verbs, *transitive, intransitive,* and *copulative* or *linking verbs.* Transitive verbs express an action that must have an object, as in "He hit the ball." Intransitive verbs express an action that is complete without an object, as in "She laughed." Linking verbs connect subjects to predicate adjectives or predicate nouns as in "He is tall" or "She became a teacher."

English verbs have *singular* and *plural* forms that must agree with the number expressed by the nouns or pronouns with which they are used. Verbs in sentences with singular subjects, with the exception of the singular personal pronouns *I* and *you,* have forms ending in *s; is, has, does, walks, talks,* and so on. Verbs appearing in sentences with plural subjects do not use the *s* ending. Complicated constructions in the subject can often make the problem of *verb agreement* a knotty one as, for example, in "Each of the team's twenty members has different ideas about the rules," where the verb must match the singularity of *each,* which is considered the simple subject of the sentence.

English verbs have six tenses, the *past, present, future, past perfect, present perfect,* and *future perfect tenses.* The simple past, present, and future tenses refer to the time that an action is performed. Perfect tenses are said to indicate the definitive completion of an action in the past, present or future. In addition, each tense has a *progressive* form, which indicates continuing action, and an emphatic form, which lays extra stress on the meaning of the verb.

English verbs are said to have four *principal parts,* from which all the tenses are formed with the help of auxiliary verbs. The principal parts are the *infinitive, present participle, past,* and *past participle.* In the case of the verb *eat,* for example, these are *eat, eating, ate,* and *eaten. Regular* verbs are those that have past and past participle forms ending in *-d* or *-ed* as with walk/walked/walked. *Irregular verbs* are those that have forms other than the regular forms as with sing/singing/sang/sung, run/running/ran/run, drive/driving/drove/driven, and so on. Lists of the principal parts of irregular verbs are listed for memorization.

English verbs have three *moods.* These are the *indicative, imperative,* and *subjunctive.* The imperative mood is used in requests or commands; the subjunctive is used for contrary-to-fact statements and in statements expressing a wish; the indicative mood is used for all other purposes. English verbs have two *voices:* the *active* and the *passive* voice. The active voice expresses an action performed by the subject; the passive voice is used when the subject receives the action of the verb. An example of the active voice is "John threw the ball." An example of the passive voice is "The ball was thrown by John."

Verb *conjugations*—or lists of forms—include considerations of person, number, voice, and tense but usually do not include all of the progressive and emphatic forms. These last forms may be suggested by including examples of the first person, singular forms as in the conjugation of the verb *see* on pages 56–57.

Auxiliary verbs, sometimes called *helping verbs,* are used in com-

CONJUGATION OF THE VERB *SEE*

Indicative Mood

	Active Voice		Passive Voice	
	Singular	*Plural*	*Singular*	*Plural*

Present Tense

Active Singular	Active Plural	Passive Singular	Passive Plural
I see	we see	I am seen	we are seen
you see	you see	you are seen	you are seen
he/she/it sees	they see	he/she/it is seen	they are seen

Present Progressive: I am seeing, and so on
Present Emphatic: I do see, and so on

Past Tense

Active Singular	Active Plural	Passive Singular	Passive Plural
I saw	we saw	I was seen	we were seen
you saw	you saw	you were seen	you were seen
he/she/it saw	they saw	he/she/it was seen	they were seen

Past Progressive: I was seeing, and so on
Past Emphatic: I did see, and so on

Future Tense

Active Singular	Active Plural	Passive Singular	Passive Plural
I shall see	we shall see	I shall be seen	we shall be seen
you will see	you will see	you will be seen	you will be seen
he/she/it will see	they will see	he/she/it will be seen	they will be seen

Future Progressive: I shall be seeing, and so on

Present Perfect Tense

I have seen	I have been seen	we have seen	we have been seen
you have seen	you have been seen	you have seen	you have been seen
he/she/it has seen	he/she/it has been seen	they have seen	they have been seen

Present Perfect Progressive: I have been seeing, and so on

Past Perfect Tense

I had seen	I had been seen	we had seen	we had been seen
you had seen	you had been seen	you had seen	you had been seen
he/she/it had seen	he/she/it had been seen	they had seen	they had been seen

Past Perfect Progressive: I had been seeing, and so on

Future Perfect Tense

I shall have seen	I shall have been seen	we shall have seen	we shall have been seen
you will have seen	you will have been seen	you will have seen	you will have been seen
he/she/it will have seen	he/she/it will have been seen	they will have seen	they will have been seen

Future Perfect Progressive: I shall have been seeing, and so on bination with the principal parts of verbs to form the various tenses. There are comparatively few auxiliary verbs, and they are usually listed along with brief definitions of the shades of meaning they bring to a combination with other verb forms. Such lists usually include the following auxiliary verbs:

is, am, are, was, were, be, being, been
have, has, had
do, does, did
shall, should, will, would, can, could, may, might, must

5. ADVERBS   An adverb modifies a verb, an adjective or another adverb. Adverbs are often described as words that tell how, where, when, and how much. Adverbs show positive, comparative, and superlative degrees, in the same ways that adjectives do, with the *-er* and-*est* endings added to some adverbs, as with soon/sooner/soonest, and some making use of periphrastic comparison as with happily/more happily/most happily. Adjectives are frequently adapted to use as adverbs by addition of an -ly ending. Some words may be used as adjectives modifying nouns, or as adverbs modifying verbs, adjectives, or other adverbs. Often the only reliable means of establishing whether a given word is to be classified as an adjective or an adverb is to consider the context in which the word appears and determine which kind of word it modifies.

The word *not* is considered to be an adverb.

6. PREPOSITIONS   A preposition is a word used to show a relationship between a noun or pronoun and some other word in a sentence. The combination of preposition plus the noun or pronoun and any modifiers the noun or pronoun may have is called a *prepositional phrase*. The noun or pronoun in the phrase is referred to as the *object of the preposition*.

7. CONJUNCTIONS   A conjunction is a word used to connect words or groups of words in sentences. The conjunctions are divided into groups identified as *coordinating, subordinating,* and *correlative* conjunctions. Coordinating conjunctions join words or groups of words that are equal in rank. Subordinating conjunctions join words or groups of words that are unequal in rank with the idea said to be of lesser or lower rank joined to one of greater or higher rank by the subordinating conjunctions. Correlative conjunctions always include two words and are used to compare or contrast parallel words or groups of words.

8. INTERJECTIONS   An interjection is a word or exclamatory sound that has no grammatical relationship to other words in a sentence. Examples are "Well!," "Oh!," and "Hurrah!"

II. Syntax

Combinations of members of the eight parts of speech categories in grammatical constructions are called *phrases, clauses,* or *sentences.*

PHRASES   When groups of words function—as a group—in the same ways that single words function, the group is called a phrase. Some clauses also function as a single part of speech.

The most common type of phrase in English is the prepositional phrase. Prepositional phrases act as modifiers of both nouns and verbs, therefore they are classed as *adjectival prepositional phrases* and *adverbial prepositional phrases,* according to the function they perform.

Other kinds of phrases and the part-of-speech functions they perform are:

1. *Participial phrases* that begin with a present participle form of a verb and function as adjectives or adverbs,

2. *Gerund phrases* that begin with a gerund and function as nouns,

3. *Infinitive phrases* that begin with the "sign of the infinitive," *to,* an infinitive form of a verb and function as nouns, adjectives or adverbs; and

4. *Appositive phrases* that are made up of nouns and their modifiers, usually appear immediately following another noun, and function as adjectives.

CLAUSES   Clauses are distinct from phrases in that they contain a subject and a verb. An *independent clause* may stand alone as a sentence. A *dependent clause,* sometimes called a *subordinate clause,* is like a phrase in that it may be described as performing the function of a single part of speech. A dependent clause is commonly—though not always—introduced by a connective word such as a subordinating conjunction or a relative pronoun. Classification of dependent clauses is made on the basis of the function it performs, the type of connective word that introduces it, or both. Some of the most common kinds of dependent clauses are:

1. *Adjective clauses* that modify nouns.

2. *Adverbial clauses* that modify verbs, adjectives or adverbs

3. *Nominal clauses* that function as nouns.

4. *Relative clauses* that function as adjectives and are usually introduced by relative pronouns.

5. *Restrictive clauses* that function as an integral part of the nominal element they modify, that is, their omission would materially change the referent of the modified word. For example, "Students *who do superior work* get good grades."

   6.   *Nonrestrictive clauses* that function as other adjectival clauses, add information about the nominal element they modify, but are not essential to establishing the exact referent of the modified word. For example, "John, *who is bright and works hard,* gets good grades."

SENTENCES   There are almost as many definitions of *sentence* as there are grammar textbooks. Most have in common the ideas that a sentence is a group of words expressing a complete thought and that a sentence contains both a *subject* and a *predicate*. A subject is that about which something is said, and a predicate is whatever is said about the subject. Subjects of simple declarative sentences are nouns or pronouns together with modifying or qualifying words. Predicates of simple declarative sentences are verbs and the words used to modify them and whatever complements appear with the verbs.

   Depending on the type of verb used, complements may or may not be required. When a complement elaborates on the meaning expressed by the noun or pronoun of the subject, it is called a *subjective complement*. If the subjective complement is an adjective, it is called a *predicate adjective;* if it is a noun, it is called a *predicate noun* or *nominal*. When a complement adds to or completes the meaning expressed by the verb, it is called an *objective complement* or *object of the verb*. *Direct objects* are said to receive the action of the verb. *Indirect objects* are those of the verb that are affected by the action of the verb but in a less immediate way. For example, in the sentence "He gave Jane a book," *book* is the direct object and *Jane* is the indirect object.

   One means of classifying sentences is according to their use or purpose. Four types are usually listed.

   1.   *Declarative sentences* make a statement.
   2.   *Imperative sentences* make requests or give commands.
   3.   *Interrogative sentences* ask questions.
   4.   *Exclamatory sentences* express strong feeling.

Another classification of sentences is on the basis of structure.

   1.   *Simple sentences* contain a single subject-predicate combination. Either the subject or the predicate or both may be compound.
   2.   *Compound sentences* contain two or more independent clauses. That is, each clause must have a subject and a predicate, and each clause must be capable of standing alone as a sentence.

3. *Complex sentences* contain an independent clause—a subject-predicate combination capable of standing alone—plus a dependent clause. Dependent or subordinate clauses have subjects, verbs, objects, and so on but are added to independent clauses in ways that allow the entire clause to function as a single part of speech. They are, therefore, incapable of standing alone as sentences. Dependent clauses may act as subjects, objects, adjectives, or adverbs.

This very brief summary of the traditional analysis of English grammar omits much of the detail to be found in many texts. Many texts disagree in their presentation of detail but the points listed here are the fundamentals usually agreed upon by traditional school grammars.

School texts making use of traditional analysis of the grammar of English place great emphasis on correct, or socially acceptable usage. Writers of such texts have always considered it their duty to help students to mastery of approved spelling, pronunciation, forms of words, and syntactic constructions.

When the first grammars of English were written, decisions as to which forms and constructions were subject to approval or rejection were usually based on analogy with Latin forms and constructions. Having elected to utilize the terminology of Latin grammar, early writers of English grammars chose also to adopt the logical principles of Latin grammar. Where English usage differed from Latin usage, it was presumed to be wrong, to need correction. In some instances, the force of English word order was so strongly opposed to the logical requirements of Latin that text writers felt compelled to point out such incorrect usage and label it. For example, English word order places objects after verbs in simple statements. English speakers therefore commonly used the objective form of the first person pronoun when making the simple statement, "It's me." Grammarians were quick to point out that the first person pronoun referred to the logical subject of the statement and, on the basis of this logic, the form demanded was the nominative and the correct statement was, therefore, "It's I."

Traditional school grammars contain profuse illustrations of ways in which English speakers frequently deviate from standards commonly accepted by the writers of the grammars. Such usages are contrasted with acceptable usages and are labeled in capital letters or boldface type:

WRONG: It's me.
RIGHT: It is I.

Over the years, standards of acceptability have shifted with the pressure of usage, but many purists still feel that any change in standards is equivalent to a lowering of standards and that any sentence spoken or written in English is either **RIGHT** or **WRONG**.

English textbooks pursue the goal of correctness in the areas of spelling, pronunciation and punctuation with almost religious fervor. All contain drills and exercises designed to instill recognition of correct and incorrect usage in the student. Where the standards of usage in the texts differ from those used consistently by the student, his family and friends, and even by the writers of current books, newspaper and magazine articles, television and motion picture scripts, the hours of drill in the English class cannot begin to compete with the "drill" of all the hours that the student participates in some kind of communicative exchange with others.

Many teachers find the task of emptying the ocean of modern grammatical "errors" with the teaspoon of traditional rules to be both frustrating and doomed to ultimate failure—some even question the desirability of doing so. They choose to spend less and less time on the study of grammar and more on the study of literature and composition. But the student who does not know something of the workings of his language does not read or write or speak—or even hear the speech of others as effectively as he might. Many textbook writers and teachers have turned to the findings of linguistic research for a more effective way of describing and teaching the grammar of English.

PART TWO

STRUCTURAL GRAMMAR

5

STRUCTURAL GRAMMAR METHODS

Reduced to the simplest possible terms, the methods of structural grammarians consist of breaking the flow of spoken language into the smallest possible units, sorting them out, and then studying the various ways in which these units are joined in meaningful combination. Structural grammarians often refer to *levels of analysis*. The concept is not a difficult one, and it is one that should be kept clearly in mind at every stage of the discussion of structural grammar. The levels are these: *phonology, morphology,* and *syntax.* The grammar of a language is a complex of systems that may be analyzed, and studied, on these three levels.

The phone and phonetic alphabets

Phonology concerns itself first with the *phones* or speech sounds of language.

A human child is born with the ability to make an infinite number of sounds. Air released from the lungs can be caused to disturb the vocal chords—as when one says "ah" for the doctor—or not—as when one heaves a sigh. The air can be channeled through the nasal passage —as with the sounds of "m" and "n"—or it can be sent through the oral cavity. When it is sent through the oral cavity, several pieces of physical apparatus can be allowed to play with it, either singly or in combination, to produce an endless number of variations. The glottis, the tongue, the teeth, and the lips may be brought into play. They rearrange themselves to form differently shaped sound or echo chambers; they may stop the air completely and then release it with a plosive sound —as with the "p" sounds in the word *paper* or the "t" sound in *time*— or they may release it slowly for sounds such as the fricative "f" of *fill* or the sibilant "s" of *sang*.

Speech sounds, like fingerprints and snowflakes, come in infinite variety. No two are precisely the same. Highly sensitive electronic equipment can detect very minute differences that are undetectable to the human ear. Nevertheless, human hearing is capable of detecting a good many differences. Because most of these distinctions are closely related to the manner in which the sounds are produced by the speaker, those who set for themselves the task of sorting human speech sounds most frequently use the parts of the speech-producing apparatus and the ways in which it is used as the basis for their sorting.

All of the equipment that we use to make the sounds of language has some other primary function. Lips, teeth, tongue, glottis, even the vocal chords and the air that stirs them, produce speech sounds as a secondary, or overlaid, function. The phonologist lists the ways that these secondary functions are performed in producing speech sounds. In simplest terms, he asks himself certain questions about each sound. First, are the vocal chords relaxed or vibrating? Second, what moves? (That is, lips, tongue, glottis, and so on.) Third, where does it go? (That is, upper teeth, lower teeth, palate, and so on.) Fourth, what happens to the air flow? (That is, momentary stoppage, slight restriction, release through the nasal passage, and so on.)

These are the conditions that produce differences in speech sounds. Listing the conditions peculiar to the production of a sound defines that sound. After a sound, or phone, is thus defined, the phonologist assigns it a symbol and places it in square brackets, [ ]. A collection of such symbols covering the full range of sounds produced by a group of human speakers is referred to as a *phonetic alphabet*.

There is a fundamental difference between this type of alphabet and, for example, the 26-letter alphabet used as the basis for English spelling. The phonetic alphabet is based on strict one-to-one correspondence between sound and symbol. Each phonetic symbol stands for a single sound. Whenever it appears in a transcription of human speech, it always stands for the same sound.

Obviously, a phonetic alphabet must contain a great many more than 26 symbols. The International Phonetic Alphabet (IPA), the most widely used of its kind, contains 20 symbols for vowels alone—as compared with the *a, e, i, o,* and *u* of the English alphabet. In addition, the IPA contains an extensive set of modifying symbols to note special qualities, such as nasality, aspiration, length, and so on, that are possible in the production of each vowel.

The phoneme and phonemic alphabets

As we have noted, normal human infants are capable of making an infinite variety of speech sounds. In the privacy of their cribs, addressing an audience of their own fingers and toes, they experiment tirelessly with their own vocal equipment. Later, they take note of those sounds which appear to convey meaning to the human beings around them. They begin to perfect their production of these sounds while, at the same time, discarding those that will not serve them. The Swahili child keeps and perfects his tongue clicks and discards guttural sounds, while the German child keeps and perfects his gutturals and discards the "th" sound. The English child learns to distinguish the difference between a "b" and a "v," while the Spanish child molds them into a combination of the two that the International Phonetic Alphabet signifies with the symbol [β]. These are only a few isolated examples of the kind of adjustment that each infant must face before he can fit comfortably into the speech community of his elders.

The phonologist who seeks to sort the sounds of a specific language and isolate the ways in which they function in that language has much in common with the child sorting his sounds. The first question is "Which sounds signal meanings within this particular language?"

Keeping to the system of sorting sounds according to the manner in which they are produced physically, the phonologist knows that many sounds that show only very small variation in their production may actually be heard as the "same" sound in a given language. He must now go a step further and, taking the various types of sounds in turn, he must attempt to determine the point at which variations cease to admit membership to one set of sounds and begin to indicate membership in another group. At which point does a difference become a signaling device within the sound system of the language? If he concentrates on the sound system of Japanese, for example, he must determine which sounds—among all those that a speaker of Japanese may produce —are important within the Japanese language system, and which small differences are considered unimportant or insignificant in signaling differences of meaning within the Japanese language.

Human speech is not made up of isolated little bursts of sound. The phonologist is aware that he has made arbitrary cuts in a steady flow of sound in order to inventory the sounds of language. He must now put the sounds back with their neighbors and see how they affect each other.

First, he seeks those combinations of sound in which all the members are alike except for one. In English, such a set of combinations might be *hit, hot,* and *hat.* The first and last sound in each case is the same; only the middle sound in each case is different. Each combination has a different meaning, and only the differences in the middle sounds can be responsible for signaling those differences of meaning. A search through the language for contrasts signaled in this way provides the phonologist with at least a part of the definition of the significant sound groups of the language. Such a significant sound group is called a *phoneme*.

Further definition of each *phoneme* is determined on the basis of how the member sounds are distributed among the other sounds of the language. An effort is made to determine how the phoneme operates when it appears as the initial sound in a combination, when it occurs after consonants, after vowels, between vowel and consonant, and so on.

For example, the sounds of English *p* show the following distributional variations: The sound of an initial *p* in English invariably involves a small plosive burst of air. A speaker can easily demonstrate this by holding one hand very close to his lips and repeating any word in English beginning with a *p*. This plosive quality may or may not be present when the *p* appears in final position; the plosive does not appear when the *p* is followed by another stop consonant, as it is in *hip boots, cupcake, map tacks*. These plosive and nonplosive variants are, therefore, in complementary distribution. Any one of the phonemes of English can be expected to have slightly varied members depending on the position it occupies in relation to other sounds. These variants are said to be *allophones,* or member phones, of a class of sounds called a phoneme. The plosive and nonplosive variants in pronouncing the *p* sounds of English are allophones of the phoneme assigned the phonemic symbol /p/. Phonemic symbols appear in slash marks to differentiate them from the bracketed phonetic symbols.

A *phonemic alphabet* of English includes symbols for those sound groups that are significant within the sound system of the English language. Each phoneme in such an alphabet represents a *group of sounds*. The sounds in each group are identified by:

1.   The fact that they are phonetically similar. That is, that they are similar in the manner in which they are produced by a speaker.

2.   The way that they operate in contrast with the members of other phonemes in similar sound environments.

3.   The fact that the various members of the group show a pattern of complementary distribution in various positions among other sounds of the language.

Consideration of the ways that these sounds operate in contrast to others may be said to mark the outer limits of a phoneme; consideration of distributional variants describe the sounds inside the phoneme boundaries.

Phonemic alphabets for different languages may have some phonemic classifications in common, but there are invariably a great many differences. A phonemic alphabet designed to classify the sounds that are significant in Modern German, for example, might be similar in some respects to a phonemic alphabet of Modern English, but the phonemic alphabet for German would contain no symbols for voiced and voiceless *th* phonemes. These sounds contrast in English—as in the words *thy* and *thigh*—but they do not operate that way in German. The German phonemic alphabet would include several vowel phonemes that do not appear in an English phonemic alphabet. Among these would be the umlaut or "rounded vowel" sounds that mark the difference in German pairs such as *mussen/müssen* and *lesen/lösen.*

A phonemic alphabet identifies the building block sounds of a language. Each language community has its own distinctive set of "blocks." Some languages have a basic set of as many as sixty of these building block sounds; others have as few as twenty. English falls approximately halfway between these two extremes.

In each case of examples given above, it was necessary to use combinations of sounds in order to show that differences of meaning do exist. The individual sounds can *signal* differences but they do not, in isolation, *carry* meaning. To return to our building block analogy, four planks of a certain size and a few nails may be required to build a window frame but they do not constitute a window frame until the planks are nailed together in a certain way. In the same way, the phonemes of a language, when combined in certain ways, acquire something that is more than the sum of their parts. For example, the English phonemes /a/, /p/, and /t/ do not carry meaning in themselves. When they are combined in a certain way, /pat/, they mean one thing; when arranged differently, /tap/, they mean something else. The meaning is a product of the *combination of phonemes,* and at this point we move on to a second system of language and a second level of language analysis. This second level is called *morphology.*

Morphology

Morphology is the study of combinations of sounds that carry single units of meaning. It is *not* the study of words or of syllables. Often a morpheme is a single word or syllable, often it is not. The difference is this: A word can best be defined as a unit of written language that, on the printed page, has a space before and after it. Examples are *cat, armadillo, ungentlemanliness.* Syllables identify the points of juncture in pronunciation. Dividing the examples above into syllables would result in *cat, ar-ma-dil-lo,* and *un-gen-tle-man-li-ness.* A morpheme is a combination of sounds that carries a single indivisible meaning. Separating the morphemes in the examples above would result in *cat, armadillo,* and *un-gentle-man-li-ness.* We will return to the matter of morphology in much greater detail later.

Syntax

Syntax, the third level of language and of structural language analysis, deals with the ways in which the single units of meaning are combined into compound and complex words, phrases, sentences or utterances, and discourse. This final and most fully meaningful step or level will also be considered in greater detail later.

It may be well to anticipate two points which are often confusing to beginning students of structural grammar.

One of these is the term *phonics* and where it fits into this study of speech sounds. Quite simply, it is another field entirely, dealing as it does with the printed or written word. Reading teachers seek to teach their students to recognize the different letters on the printed page and assign sounds to each. They are working in the opposite direction from the phonologist. The teacher works from the printed symbol to the sound. The phonologist isolates the sounds of speech and assigns symbols to those sounds. There is, in phonology, a one-to-one correspondence between sound and symbol. As any reader of English can attest, this is not true in reverse. The English spelling system does not boast one-to-one correspondence and teachers of phonics must face the task of explaining that fact as effectively as possible to their students. For the moment, we will leave the reading teachers to their tasks.

A second point of confusion arises from the fact that most beginning students of structural grammar bring with them a knowledge of the system of pronunciation symbols and diacritical marks originated by Noah Webster and used in most of the dictionaries printed in America for many years. More recent dictionaries, including the *Webster's Third New International Dictionary,* have begun to change over to at least some use of the International Phonetic Alphabet. For those accustomed to the older system, some adjustment is necessary. Since many of the same symbols are used, but some are used in slightly different ways, it is best not to attempt to equate the two systems. For example, when making notations from the vowel charts included here, it is best to make use of examples of words in which the vowel appears rather than adding diacritical marks from dictionary footnotes.

For a clearer understanding of the structuralist approach to the phonology of English, it is safer to put both Mr. Webster and the whole matter of phonics on the shelf for a while.

6

THE PHONOLOGY
OF ENGLISH

Investigation of the sounds of human speech is a field that has had a long and varied history. George Trager and Henry Lee Smith, Jr., whose work has been most influential among American structuralists, owe much to their predecessors. Some of the background can be left to your own independent study. Some is important for purposes of clarity here.

The International Phonetic Association was formed by a group of modern language teachers in Europe in the latter part of the nineteenth century. The association's principal objective was to classify and categorize the speech sounds of all the languages they taught. Such classification would provide means of more effective teaching of native pronunciation of other languages to their students. They recognized the need for some system that allowed for one-to-one correspondence between sound and symbol. The complex system devised to meet this need is called the International Phonetic Alphabet, or, more commonly, the IPA. It is the best known and most widely used of all phonetic alphabets. Others designed for use in working with a specific language or group of languages are often adaptations of the IPA. Such phonetic alphabets are the primary tools of linguists who search out and record the speech sounds of a language as a basis for their description of that language.

The idea that within any given speech community, certain sets of sounds were heard as "the same" had achieved wide recognition by the 1940s. The most influential application of the idea to an analysis of the speech sounds of English was *An Outline of English Structure* published by Trager and Smith in 1951. After a dozen years of painstaking research, they had arrived at a phonemic alphabet for English that recognized 45 phonemes, or significant sounds, in the language. Their highly detailed consideration of each phoneme group included evidence of their function as contrastive signals in the language, the listing of nonsignificant variants and their distribution patterns, regional variations, and sound clusters or combinations. They also dealt with larger patterns made up of English phonemes. Their work has formed the basis of much of the structuralist analysis of the phonemic system of the English language ever since.

The Trager-Smith phonemic alphabet makes use of symbols that are similar to IPA phonetic symbols for consonants and vowels to designate many of the phonemes of English. Differences are primarily in the use of more commonly used printing symbols wherever possible.

THE CONSONANT AND GLIDE PHONEMES OF ENGLISH

The phonemes of English may be classified, as phones are classified, according to the physical means of their production.

The consonant phonemes, then, are said to be distinguished by (1) whether or not they are voiced, (2) the articulators used in their production, (3) the points of articulation used in their production, and (4) the degree to which the flow of air is constricted as the sound is made.

ARTICULATORS AND POINTS OF ARTICULATION

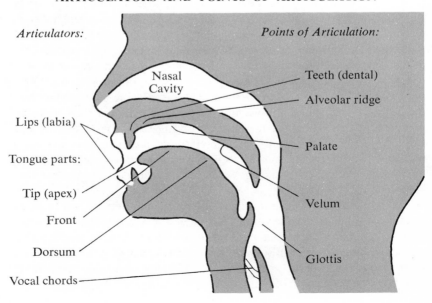

Articulators:

Lips (labia)

Tongue parts:

Tip (apex)

Front

Dorsum

Vocal chords

Nasal Cavity

Points of Articulation:

Teeth (dental)

Alveolar ridge

Palate

Velum

Glottis

The diagram on page 72 locates articulators and points of articulation. The terms derived from the names of the parts of the human speech mechanism are used to define the various speech sounds produced.

Voicing

Contrast between voiced and voiceless qualities of consonants can be demonstrated by saying the words *pip, pop, bib,* and *bob* aloud. In the first two, voicing is confined to the vowel sound; in the second two, voicing is a part of both consonant and vowel sounds. Thus, /p/ is a voiceless consonant; /b/ a voiced one.

Constriction of air flow

The terms below refer to the quality of the sound produced based upon the degree to which the air is constricted.

Stops The flow of air is stopped completely as with /p, b, t, d, k, g/

Fricatives The flow of air is forced through an almost closed space as with /f, v, θ, ð/

Affricates These are a combination of stop plus fricative as with the consonant sounds of *church* and *judge,* /č, ǰ/

Sibilants The flow of air is forced through an almost closed space involving the teeth, /s, z, š, ž/

Lateral The flow of air is channeled around the tongue, /l/

Nasals The flow of air is forced through the nasal cavity as with /m, n, ŋ/.

Glides These are sometimes called *semivowels* because they are similar to vowels in that the flow of air is not impeded and differences in sound are made by changing the shape of the oral cavity by manipulating the tongue and lips. Because their distribution throughout the language is more like consonants than vowels and because —at least in the case of /y/ and /w/—their sounds cannot be sustained as other vowel sounds can be, they are usually grouped with the consonants. The term *glide* is more specific since it recognizes the fact that the tongue moves as each sound is produced. English glide phonemes are the retroflex glide /r/, and /h, y, w/.

GIVING NAMES TO PHONEMES   Terms that combine the distinctive characteristics of each of the consonants of the English phonemic system are these:

Phonemic Symbol	Voicing	Articulator	Point of Articulation	Constriction of Air Flow
/p/	voiceless		bilabial	stop
/b/	voiced		bilabial	stop
/t/	voiceless	apico-	alveolar	stop
/d/	voiced	apico-	alveolar	stop
/k/	voiceless	dorso-	velar	stop
/g/	voiced	dorso-	velar	stop
/f/	voiceless	labio-	dental	fricative
/v/	voiced	labio-	dental	fricative
/θ/	voiceless	apico-	dental	fricative
/ð/	voiced	apico-	dental	fricative
/č/	voiceless	apico-	alveolar	affricate
/ǰ/	voiced	apico-	alveolar	affricate
/s/	voiceless	apico-	alveolar	sibilant
/z/	voiced	apico-	alveolar	sibilant
/š/	voiceless	fronto-	palatal	sibilant
/ž/	voiced	fronto-	palatal	sibilant
/m/	*		bilabial	nasal
/n/		apico-	alveolar	nasal
/ŋ/		dorso-	velar	nasal
/l/		apico-	alveolar	lateral
/r/	voiced	** apico-	alveolar	glide
/y/	voiced	fronto-	palatal	glide
/w/	voiced	dorso-	palatal	glide
/h/	voiceless		glottal	glide

* nasals and laterals are all voiced and this is usually omitted in referring to them.

** an alternate term that is most frequently used is retroflex glide.

Each of the complex-looking terms is made up of four parts which define the phoneme in terms of (1) voicing, (2) articulator, (3) point of articulation, and (4) the degree to which the air flow is constricted. The terms are not so forbidding if each is first considered part-by-part and then as a combination. Note that sets of stops are listed first, then fricatives, affricates, sibilants, and so on, with each set listed as they are articulated, front to back, in the mouth.

THE VOWEL PHONEMES OF ENGLISH

The vowel phonemes of English are distinguished by the position of the arch of the tongue as each is made.

The vowel symbols are often shown in nine squares but it would seem more true to English usage to show them in nine overlapping circles since many speakers of English use dialects that shift the whole system in one direction or another. Borderline vowels are not easy to classify unless taken in the context of the speaker's other vowel sounds. These borderline vowels are sometimes said to be "in free variation." The fact that there is some variation of this type does not alter the fact that there is an English vowel system and that the distinctions shown above are a useful means of describing it. Vowels are referred to by position. The /e/ is the *middle front vowel,* the /ɔ/ is the *low back vowel,* and so on.

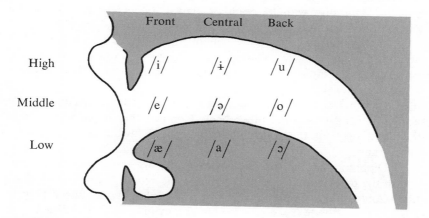

The arch of the tongue is shown here in position to produce the mid-central vowel, which is often called the *schwa,* and is assigned the symbol /ə/.

Read aloud the illustrative words given on the chart of sound symbols on pages 79–80, noting as you do the position of your tongue at the sound of each vowel. Compare them with the distinctions shown on the diagram above.

One means of demonstrating the contrastive nature of these vowel phonemes is to substitute the sounds, one by one, into the same frame of consonant sounds. For example, sequences such as /pit/, /pet/, /pæt/, /put/, /pat/ and /mis/, /mes/, /mæs/, /mas/, /mɔs/, /mus/ may be produced. These phonemic transcriptions occasionally match standard English spelling; more often, they do not. In the case of /mas/ and /mɔs/ above, they represent dialect differences in the pronunciation of the English word *moss.* Dictionary markings may cause confusion here. For examples, some dictionaries consider the vowel sound of *ride* to be a "long i" and mark it ī. In actual fact, the sound is not a long anything. The only way to produce the sound is to move the tongue, which produces a diphthong.

English speakers make use of a large number of diphthongs. Diphthongs are blends of two sounds or, more specifically, sounds which cannot be located by a single tongue position because the tongue moves as they are being pronounced. Undaunted by this perversity of English tongues, the phonologists have assigned such diphthongs two symbols. The first indicates the position of the tongue when the sound begins and the second records the direction in which it moves. This practice has a distinct advantage over the alternative, which would be to assign a long list of additional symbols to each possible diphthong combination.

For the second symbol in diphthongs, the IPA and some structuralists use a second vowel symbol. In effect they combine the tongue's point of departure with its point of arrival. Others prefer to use the glide symbol that indicates the fact that movement does occur.

Diphthongs using the glide symbol /y/ are those that begin with a middle, low or back vowel and move forward. Contrast the simple vowels with the diphthongs in the following pairs: /rat/, /rayt/; /red/, /reyd/; /ɔl/, /ɔyl/.

Diphthongs using the glide symbol /w/ are those that begin with a high or front vowel and move back. Contrast the simple vowels with the diphthongs in the following pairs: /fil/, /fiwl/; /bæt/, /bæwt/; /ha/, /haw/.

Diphthongs using the glide symbol /h/ are those that begin with any of the outer vowels and move toward the center /ə/, or schwa position. Contrast the simple vowels with the diphthongs in the following pairs: /kat/, /kaht/; /kan/, /kahlm/; /aydɨl/, /aydɨhl/. There are often dialectical differences in the pronunciation of these diphthongs. The phonemic transcriptions here represent the writer's pronunciation of the words *cot, caught, con, calm, idyl,* and *ideal.*

Retroflex /r/ is also usually considered among the diphthongs because it has the effect of coloring any vowel that precedes it. Diphthongs using the glide symbol /r/ are those that begin with any of the vowels that dissolve into a retroflex (or backward) movement of the tip of the tongue. Note the quality of the vowels in words like /bɨrd/ and /kart/.

Studies of the phonology of English include noting the frequency of certain patterns, sound combinations that do not occur in English, sound combinations that do not appear initially in English words, and many other details of the sound system of English.

The chart of IPA and Trager-Smith symbols on pages 79–80 demonstrates some of the areas where phonetic symbols (those for phones) and phonemic symbols are the same as well as some of the areas where they differ.

THE INTONATION PHONEMES OF ENGLISH

There are still other phonemes in the English sound system, other factors in the pronunciation of the language, that provide signals of differences in meaning. These are not so easily identifiable as the consonants and vowels; they are even more difficult to assess in other languages.

One of the most difficult problems in learning a second language is the matter of picking up the melody of the language. We usually are not aware of our own failures in this area, but the difficulties of others who may be learning English as a second language are always apparent to the native speaker of English. The lilt of the Irish or the melody of Spanish, for example, very often superimpose themselves on the English with a charming but undeniably noticeable effect.

The factors that are involved in this melody of language are those we are concerned with when we speak of the *intonation* phonemes of *stress, pitch,* and *juncture.*

The following examples will demonstrate the reasons for classifying these factors as phonemes in the English sound system.

Stress refers to the volume of sound allotted to the various segments of an utterance. They are akin to the accented syllables of dictionaries. Most structuralists recognize four degrees of stress. These, together with their symbols, are: primary, /´/; secondary, /ˆ/; tertiary, /`/; and weak, /˘/. Examples of how stress works as a contrastive phoneme in English are the following pairs: gréenhòuse, grèen hóuse; shórtstòp, shòrt stóp; Frènch téachĕr, Frénch tèachĕr.

Pitch, as with musical pitch, deals with the tone—how high or low the voice is—which is determined by the degree of tension of the vocal chords. Most structuralists recognize four levels of pitch in English. These are usually numbered 1 to 4, low to high. Some superimpose lines over example sentences to indicate rising and falling pitch; some make use of little arrows, ⟋ ↓ ⟍ , for this purpose. Examples of how pitch works as a contrastive phoneme in English can be seen in the following sentences: "How is your brother Tom?" and "How is your brother, Tom?" In written language the difference between the two sentences is indicated by the comma in the second sentence; in speech the difference is indicated by differences in stress and pitch. Reading the sentences aloud will demonstrate how the contrast works for you.

Juncture refers to the breaks or pauses in the flow of speech. Most structuralists recognize four lengths of juncture. The symbols for these, from shortest to longest, are: +, ⟋, //, and #. These are primarily useful for analysis of longer passages of speech, of sounds in larger contexts, but juncture can be shown to be a contrastive phoneme in English with the comparison of such pairs as *night rate* and *nitrate* or *I scream* and *ice cream.*

These phonemes of stress, pitch and juncture are often called the *suprasegmental* phonemes because they are a part of the melodic overlay of speech. In phonemic transcription they are written above the symbols for sound segments.

The analysis of the phonemic system of English presented here includes forty-five phonemes:

24 consonants, including the glides
 9 vowels
 4 degrees of stress
 4 levels of pitch
 4 lengths of juncture

There is some slight variation from structuralist to structuralist; but with a reasonable grasp of these symbols and the rationale behind them, the slight differences to be found among structuralists will present no great difficulty. Without some such basis for understanding, it is difficult if not impossible to make use of any book on structural grammar because the writers make extensive use of examples that have been transcribed into these—or very similar—sound symbols.

Those who approach structural analysis of the phonemic structure of the English language for the first time are often intimidated by the flood of new concepts, new terminology and the fact that there seem to be no hard and fast sound categories, especially where the English vowels are concerned.

It is true that rigidly defined sound categories would eliminate ambiguity and misunderstanding among speakers of the language, but they would also eliminate many of the sources of beauty in our poetry and of laughter in our humor.

The speaker of English is capable of great flexibility in classifying the sounds that he hears. An excellent example of this is to be found in the comic *Anguish Languish* stories and verses composed by Howard Chace. How much trouble do you have in interpreting "Ladle Rat Rotten Hut?" (For best results read the story aloud with the intonation pattern of the fairy tale—another indication of how important stress, pitch and juncture are to the phonemic structure of English!)

LADLE RAT ROTTEN HUT *

Wants pawn term dare worsted ladle gull hoe lift wetter murder inner ladle cordage honor itch offer lodge, dock, florist. Disk ladle gull orphan worry putty ladle rat cluck

---

* From *Anguish Languish,* by H. L. Chace, copyright, 1953 by Howard Chace. Reprinted by permission.

wetter ladle rat hut, and fur disk raisin pimple colder Ladle Rat Rotten Hut.

Wan moaning Ladle Rat Rotten Hut's murder colder inset, "Ladle Rat Rotten Hut, heresy ladle basking winsome burden barter an shirker cockles. Tick disk ladle basking tutor cordage offer groin-murder hoe lifts honor udder site offer florist. Shaker lake! Dun stopper laundry wrote! Dun stopper peck floors! Dun daily-doily inner florist, an yonder nor sorghum stenches, dun stopper torque wet strainers!"

"Hoe-cake, murder," resplendent Ladle Rat Rotten Hut, an tickle ladle basking an stuttered oft.

Honor wrote tutor cordage offer groin-murder, Ladle Rat Rotten Hut mitten anomalous woof. . . .

The rest of the story, along with other, similar stories and verses, is to be found in Professor Chace's book *Anguish Languish,* published by Prentice-Hall in 1956.

CHART OF SOUND SYMBOLS

Consonants

	T-S	IPA	As in:	Transcriptions
Stops:	/p/	—	pit	/pit/
	/t/	—	tip	/tip/
	/k/	—	cake	/keyk/
	/b/	—	bit	/bit/
	/d/	—	dip	/dip/
	/g/	—	get	/get/
Affricates:	/č/	[tʃ]	choke	/čok/ [tʃok]
	/ǰ/	[dʒ]	joke	/ǰok/ [dʒok]
Fricatives:	/f/	—	fit	/fit/
	/v/	—	van	/væn/
	/θ/	—	thigh	/θay/
	/ð/	—	thy	/ðay/
Sibilants:	/s/	—	sit	/sit/
	/š/	[ʃ]	shame	/šeym/ [ʃem]
	/z/	—	zoo	/zuw/
	/ž/	[ʒ]	vision	/vižən/ [vɪʒən]
Nasals:	/m/	—	met	/met/
	/n/	—	net	/net/
	/ŋ/	—	sing	/siŋ/
Lateral:	/l/	—	let	/let/
Glides:	/r/	—	rate	/reyt/
	/y/	[j]	yet	/yet/ [jɛt]
	/w/	—	wet	/wet/
	/h/	—	hate	/heyt/
	/wh/	[ʍ]	whale	/wheyl/ [ʍel]

CHART OF SOUND SYMBOLS (Continued)

Vowels

T-S	IPA	As in:	Transcriptions
/a/	[ɑ]	father	/faðər/ [fɑðɚ]
/æ/	—	bat	/bæt/
/e/	[ɛ]	bet	/bet/ [bɛt]
/i/	[ɪ]	pit	/pit/ [pɪt]
/ɨ/	—	pitted	/pitɨd/ [pɪtɨd]
/ə/	—	love	/ləv/
/u/	[ʊ]	put	/put/ [pʊt]
/o/	—	hotel	/hotel/ [hotɛl]
/ɔ/	—	bought	/bɔt/

Examples of sounds considered to be simple vowels by IPA, diphthongs by T-S:

/ah/	[a]	half	/hahf/ [haf]
/iy/	[i]	beat	/biyt/ [bit]
/ey/	[e]	bait	/beyt/ [bet]
/ow/	[o]	boat	/bowt/ [bot]
/uw/	[u]	boot	/buwt/ [but]
/ɨr/	[ɝ]	bird	/bɨrd/ [bɝt]

Examples of sounds considered to be diphthongs by both IPA and T-S:

/ay/	[ɑɪ]	fight	/fayt/ [fɑɪt]
/aw/	[aʊ]	cow	/kaw/ [kaʊ]
/oy/	[ɔi]	boy	/boy/ [bɔi]

NOTE: This chart follows the common practice of placing T-S transcriptions in slash marks, those of IPA in brackets. Where dashes appear, they indicate IPA uses same symbol as T-S for that sound.

$$\underline{7}$$

THE MORPHOLOGY
OF ENGLISH

It is sometimes difficult for teachers of English to adapt their thinking to the methods used by the structuralist. The structuralist thinks in terms of the spoken language while the teacher has become so oriented to methods steeped in the printed word that it has become almost a conditioned reflex for him to think of all language study in that light. It therefore seems worth stating again that one of the most basic of all differences between the traditional and structural approaches is that traditional methods of grammatical analysis are based upon examination of examples drawn from the literature and other writings of a given language, while the methods of structural grammarians insist upon the primacy of speech.

This difference must be kept clearly in mind as we consider the second level of structural analysis, *morphology*. When the structuralist speaks of *morphs, morphemes,* and *allomorphs,* those who think primarily in terms of written language wonder why he doesn't simply call them "words" and have done with it. The reason he does not do so is that he is not talking about words.

For the moment, in order to put our conditioned reflexes at rest, it is best to force ourselves into the frame of reference from which the structuralist works. It is difficult for an untrained native speaker to make a completely objective analysis of spoken English. Indeed, it is sometimes difficult even for trained linguists to be completely objective in working with their own language. We will, therefore, concern ourselves with an imaginary language.

This imaginary language is one of the Polynesian family of languages and is spoken by the inhabitants of a South Pacific island. It has no written form.

We shall assume that we have recorded long passages of the speech of these people using phonetic symbols. There are, of course, points of juncture in these transcriptions; but there is no reason to believe that these mark off words any more than that there are significant pauses between words in normal English speech. We have simply set the phonetic symbols down with junctures but without spaces across the page. We have noted those phone types that seem to signal meaning, noted those that seem capable of free substitution, and constructed at least a working outline of the phonemic structure of the language.

Our next step is to discover the recurring combinations of phonemes which obviously carry units of meaning among speakers of this language. We may not assign to these combinations the designation of words for the very good reason that some may be inflections, suffixes, or prefixes—they may recur and they may carry some kind of meaning but they will not stand alone as words. Other forms may, indeed, eventually be found to be words, but for this stage of our analysis we need a term that will apply to combinations of sound that carry meaning, regardless of whether they stand alone or not. The term structuralists use is *morph*.

We may find that our passages of transcribed speech contain a morph made up of the segments /glúb/ and others of the same segments with slightly different intonation, /glùb/ and /glûb/. We may assume for the moment that the speakers intended the same notion with each of these and that they are then allomorphs of the same morpheme—that is, that their differences are not significant at this level of analysis. Their intonation phonemes are said to be "in free variation." There is, in our Polynesian language, a {glub} morpheme. We do not know what meaning it carries but it probably carries *some* meaning. Now we find that in several instances the segments /glub/—whatever their stress pattern—are followed by the segments /ɨt/ and that other recurring patterns also have /ɨt/ immediately following them. They fall into larger patterns in much the same way. We assume, then, that we have isolated another morpheme, the {ɨt} morpheme, which may be an inflection or a suffix of some other type.

Further along in our sorting, it appears that each of the allomorphs of {glub}, and therefore the morpheme {glub} itself, has a concrete referent. It is, in traditional terms, a noun. The {ɨt} morpheme may then indicate something about nouns that the speakers of this language consider important in communicating their thoughts. Its function may be to indicate gender or plurality or something vital to them although completely outside our system. The only way to define it is to examine every single occurrence of the {ɨt} morpheme and, on the basis of its behavior, make generalizations. We can then procure other samples of the Polynesian language and see if our newly formed hypothesis works consistently as we have theorized. If it does so, we may state it as a rule of that language. This, quite obviously, is what is meant by the application of scientific method to the study of language.

In the Polynesian language, a *glub* may be a head covering and the {ɨt} morpheme may indicate more than one. In English a head covering is a hat and we indicate more than one by adding an /s/. We know this and perhaps it seems pointless to go through the steps of scientific method to discover something that is so obvious. But suppose we can formulate a statement that a given class of linguistic forms is set apart —at least in part—by the fact that the members of that class will admit a morpheme of plurality. Then at least a part of the definition of a noun may become "a word that will show number." It is certainly a more precise means of definition than "a noun is the name of a thing."

With this very sketchy justification—one that will be elaborated upon at some length later—we return to the terms morph, allomorph, and morpheme and the concepts they designate.

A *morph* is a combination of sounds that carries a single, indivisible meaning. The form /buk/ contains a single morph; the form /buks/ contains two—/buk/ plus /-s/, which carries another meaning, that of plurality. The form /æct/ contains one morph; the form /æktɨd/ contains two—/ækt/ plus /-ɨd/, which carries a meaning of time other than the present. The form /ǰɨræf/ is a single morph and so is /mækərownɨ/. The form /spɨndəl/ contains two morphs—/spɨn/ and /dəl/. The meaning of /dəl/ in this form is not easy to specify. The structuralist does not concern himself with that problem at this level of analysis but is content to know that the meaning is there. He bases this judgment on the recurrence of the /-dəl/ morphs in such forms as *handle, treadle,* and *paddle.*

Morpheme is a collective term for a family of linguistic forms that are semantically similar and in complementary distribution. Notice that this definition does not include phonemic similarity. For example, the plural morpheme in English, which may be designated by the cover symbol {Z₁}, has principal allomorphs /-s/, /-z/, and /-ɨz/ as in /buks/, /bedz/, and /dɨšɨz/, but it also includes a few occurrences of /ən/ as in /aksən/, /∅/ or "zero" allomorph, as in /šiyp/, and some instances of internal vowel change, as in /mays/. These last allomorphs are not exceptions but a part of the rule in its complete statement since no noun in Standard English admits more than one of the various forms. That is, we may say *oxen,* but not **oxes;* two *sheep,* but not two **sheeps; mice,* but not **mouses.* Thus the allomorphs of the plural morpheme $\{Z_1\}$ are semantically similar—each carries the notion of more than one— and they are in complementary distribution—as one structuralist puts it, "they do not get in each other's way."

Irregular plurals do exist in English, but listing all nouns in the language together with their plurals would demonstrate the overwhelming numbers of those making use of the regular allomorphs /-s/, /-z/, and /-ɨz/. When a child makes the mistake of saying "My foots are cold," he is only trying to force the noun *foot* into a regular pattern that he already recognizes. The names of all his body parts, except for *tooth* and *foot,* form plurals in regular ways. When the child is corrected by an adult, he frequently incorporates the vowel change in this way: "My feets are cold." He is still doggedly, if unconsciously, attempting to make the plural fit the system of regular English plurals.

The systematic workings of the regular allomorphs of the plural morpheme throughout the language can be stated quite simply. The regular allomorphs /-s/, /-z/, and /-ɨz/ are distributed according to the final sound of the form to which they are attached:

/-s/	appears after morphs ending in the voiceless consonants /p, t, k, f, θ/
/-z/	appears after morphs ending in all vowels and after voiced consonants /b, d, g, v, ð, m, n, ŋ, l/ and after the semi-vowels /r, y, w, h/
/-ɨz/	appears after consonants having sibilant or affricative qualities /s, š, č, z, ž, ǰ/

This kind of regularity in the language lends itself particularly well to discovery methods of teaching. Children find it as fascinating as the most dedicated structural linguistic scholar.

An *allomorph,* then, is one of the member forms of a given morpheme. The plural morpheme symbol $\{Z_1\}$ is written in braces to designate it as a cover term. The subscript $_1$ differentiates it from the $\{Z_2\}$ morpheme which carries the meaning of the possessive case for nouns, and the $\{Z_3\}$ morpheme which operates with the third person singular form of verbs. Among the allomorphs of the $\{Z_1\}$, or plural morpheme, are /-s/, /-z/, /-ɨz/, /ən/ and /Ø/.

This method of classifying morphemes has much in common with methods of classifying phonemes.

Phonemic Classification

Morphemic Classification

Phones are unique units of sound.

Morphs are combinations of sound that *carry* a single indivisible meaning.

Allophones are member phones of a phoneme. They are similar in the way that they are produced and the variants show a pattern of complementary distribution in relation to other phones.

Allomorphs are member morphs of a morpheme. They may or may not be similar in sound, but they do show a pattern of complementary distribution among other morphs.

Phoneme is a group of phones, all of which operate as a device for *signaling* differences of meaning within the sound system of a language.

Morpheme is a group of morphs, all of which carry the same meaning within the morphemic system of a language.

Other terms that the structuralist finds useful are *bound morpheme* and *free morpheme.* A free morpheme is one which may stand alone as an independent linguistic form, such as *man, go, call,* or may combine with other morphemes, as with *manly, going, called.* Bound morphemes are those which must always appear as part of a combination of forms. Examples are *-ly, -ing, -ed, de-,* and *in-.*

When working with combinations of morphemes, the structuralist seeks first to designate the morpheme or morphemes that carry the principal semantic load. These basic forms he calls, sensibly enough, *bases.* Forms added to bases that in some way qualify or modify the meaning of the bases, he calls *affixes.*

In English a base may be—and usually is—a free morpheme, a form that is capable of standing alone. (This is in contrast to Latin, for example, in which most bases are bound morphemes.) English contains a comparatively small number of bases that are bound morphemes, or forms that will not stand alone as words. Still other bases may be combinations of morphemes.

In the case of a base that is a bound morpheme, the meaning is usually not easily isolated. Nevertheless, we do see some notional similarity in such forms as de-*sist,* re-*sist,* sub-*sist;* con-*clude,* ex-*clude,* pre-*clude,* in-*clude,* oc-*clude;* and re-*ceive,* per-*ceive,* de-*ceive.*

Affixes have no free allomorphs (though some have homophones as with *in* and *in-*) and must always appear with a base. They are, therefore, always bound morphemes. Affixes attached to the beginning of other forms are called *prefixes;* those attached to the end of other forms are called *suffixes.*

At last we come to the structural linguist's definition of a word. A *word* is a linguistic form which consists of a base with or without one or more affixes.

The workings of affixes are divided into two broad categories: *inflection* and *derivation*. *Inflectional suffixes* adapt words to grammatical functions without changing lexical meanings. The referents of *boy, cat,* and *house* are not changed by adding a plural morpheme. The notion of *carry, try,* or *drop* is not changed by adding an *-ed* that indicates tense. Contrast these with the differences made by adding *derivational suffixes* which alter the lexical meaning, often the part of speech, when they are added to another form: *happy/happiness, act/actor, friend/friendship, paint/painter.* The second word in each pair is said to be derived from the first, thus the term derivational suffix. Notice that this use of the term *derived* has nothing to do with historical derivation, but simply refers to the word-building functions of certain affixes in English.

Further means of distinguishing between inflectional and derivational affixes in English have been listed below in outline form in order to facilitate contrast and comparison.

I. Suffixes may be either inflectional or derivational.

  A. Inflectional suffixes:
    1. Must *always* come at the end of a word or morpheme group. (An apparent exception is the possessive plural of nouns where one, either the possessive or the plural, is almost always the /∅/ allomorph. In a few very rare instances such as *men's, children's,* both occur.)
    2. Have very wide distribution.
      a) Almost every noun in the language takes inflectional endings for the plural and the possessive.
      b) Almost all verbs show tense.
      c) Most adjectives and adverbs show the comparative and superlative degrees.
    3. Tend to be regular in their distribution.
    4. Other, related terms: inflection, inflected forms, inflectional paradigms.

  B. Derivational suffixes:
    1. May or may not be followed by other suffixes. They may be followed by other derivational suffixes or by inflectional suffixes.
    2. Have more limited use and distribution is less regular. For example, *-ment* may not be added to all verbs to produce nouns as it does in *agreement.* Other suffixes

used for this purpose include *-ance, -al, -ation* as in such forms as *disturbance, accrual, accusation.*

3. Are not regular in use. The attempt to force them into regular use can result in such statements as "Hamlet's unableness to overcome his undecidedness . . ."
4. Other, related terms: derivation, derivative, derivational paradigm.

Examples of both types of suffixes: friend, friend*s*, friend'*s*, friendly, friendli*est*, friendli*er*, friendliness, friendship, friendship*s*, friendless, friendlessness.

II. Prefixes. These are *always* derivational. At one time English had inflectional prefixes, such as the ge- participle, but none has survived into modern English.)

Add to the examples above: befriend, befriend*ed*, unfriendly, unfriend-li*er*, unfriendli*est*. Note that in the case of each italicized suffix in both lists of examples, the suffix is an inflectional one and comes last. Each of the affixes that is not italicized, the derivational suffixes and prefixes, changes the lexical meaning, frequently even the part of speech category of the form to which they are added.

Because the derivational affixes have the force to alter the lexical meaning of the forms to which they are added and because they come first, they are considered to be a more basic level of structure. This is demonstrated by the form *dis-agree-ment-s* in which the *s*, considered a later level of structure, forms the plural of all the collective meanings of the first three morphemes.

Charting the morphemic system of English in the same way that we charted the phonemic system is a tremendously complicated undertaking. Listing all of the combinations of sound that carry a single meaning and classifying them into bases, inflectional suffixes, derivational prefixes, and suffixes would result in a very long list.

It is possible to chart the types of forms and the ways in which they may be combined using the terminology of the structuralist.

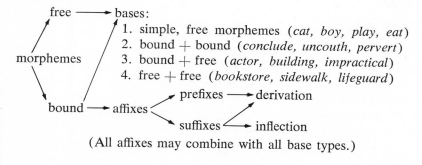

(All affixes may combine with all base types.)

8

STRUCTURAL ANALYSIS OF ENGLISH SYNTAX

The speaker of English makes use of a system of sounds. His method of combining these sounds into meaningful linguistic forms also follows a system. These—the phonemic and morphemic systems of English—may be similar to the systems of a few other languages, but they are not exactly like any other language. The syntax of English— the third level of grammar and the third level of analysis—deals with the more complex combinations of linguistic forms. It, too, is unique to English.

Most structuralists agree that syntax begins with the defining of word classes. Certain words in English do have referents or lexical meaning. The study of this kind of meaning, according to the structuralist, belongs to the writer of dictionaries, the semanticist and the psycholinguist. But words have another kind of meaning—the meaning that they take on in combination with other words. The structural grammarian, then, is primarily concerned with this aspect of language, which is yet another system.

The forms that English words may be given and the sequences in which they are arranged with other words to express larger, more complex meanings make up the syntactic pattern or system of English. Identification of a word class is not, then, a matter of "What do these words mean?" but "How do they fit into a pattern?" "What forms will they take?" and "How do they behave in combination with other forms?"

The devices used by structuralists for establishing word classes in English include consideration of ways in which certain types of words can be grouped into sets, called *paradigms,* on the basis of the inflectional and derivational affixes that they will take; consideration of how these forms are positioned in relation to other forms in sentences, and analysis of intonation patterns that are peculiar to certain groupings of forms.

Some words in English may not make use of the first of these structural devices. They have no inflectional or derivational endings. They are simply tools for putting other words together. They perform a function in the system—outside the system they have little or no meaning whatever. What, for example, is the meaning of *because, the, and,* or *very?* These words fall into categories determined only on the basis of their position in grammatical structures and the intonation patterns of the combinations they enter into. They are referred to by the collective term *function words.* The categories of function words are often called closed classes because new forms are rarely, if ever, added to them. New nouns, verbs, and adjectives are frequently borrowed or coined by speakers of English. There is, for example, the steady flow of new words into the language as a result of the space program. But the lists of prepositions, conjunctions, and other types of function words in English are firmly established.

Some function words operate so closely with certain classes of words in English that they serve as still another means of identifying those classes. The *noun determiners* (*a, an, the, my, your, our, their*), for example, are always followed by nouns and are, therefore, a useful means of identifying nouns.

Function words represent only a few hundred of the more than half million words in English. All of the remainder may be sorted into a few major *form classes* on the basis of the structural criteria discussed below.

1. INFLECTIONAL PARADIGMS These are sets of forms. Each set is made up of a base form and the base form plus whatever morphemic changes—either the addition of suffixes or sound changes or both—may be used to adapt the base form to certain functions without changing their lexical meaning. For example, the inflectional paradigm for one form class, nouns, is made up of a base, or singular, form and the base form plus plural, possessive, and possessive plural inflections.

2. DERIVATIONAL PARADIGMS These are made up of sets of endings that may be attached to bases that may shift their lexical meaning or part of speech or both. Some examples of noun-marking derivational suffixes are *-hood, -ship, -ness,* and *-ment.* Words having these endings are recognized, even in isolation, as nouns.

3. POSITION OR WORD ORDER Word classes are usually identifiable on the basis of where they appear in a given sentence. Many words are not recognizable as a single part of speech when they are met in isolation. We do not need to depend on the structuralists for proof of

this but may rely on *Webster's Collegiate Dictionary,* which lists the word *round,* for example, as adjective, noun, transitive verb, preposition, and adverb. In order to isolate the definition that you seek, you must have the word in a context. You must, in short, rely on word order.

4. INTONATION PATTERNS   Contrasts made by differences in stress, pitch and juncture often identify a form as belonging to one word class or another. For example, the difference between the noun *contract* and the verb *contract,* or the difference made in the sentence "The man tore up the street" when greater juncture is before or after the form *up,* is determined by differences in intonation pattern.

5. FUNCTION WORDS   Limited numbers of these forms work with certain form classes to signal relationships and classes. For example, the sentence "Box leaves before you go" is ambiguous unless the noun determiner *the* is inserted before *box* or before *leaves.*

Some structuralists maintain that some English form class words may be either noun, verb, or adjective—as with *fancy*—and should be classified as noun-verb-adjectives; that some are either noun or verb—as with *man*—and should be classed as noun-verbs, and so on. Others maintain that it is more orderly to establish criteria for form classes and, if a word fits more than one, simply consider that there is a noun *fancy* as in "Good-by, my fancy," a verb *fancy* as in "She may fancy the red dress," and an adjective *fancy* as in "It was a very fancy dress." Since school grammars generally follow the latter practice, we will explore it in greater detail.

Because their methods differ from those of traditional grammarians, structuralists arrive at classifications that are somewhat different from those of traditional grammar. Traditional terminology must be adapted to slightly different uses and augmented when new concepts are introduced. Some structuralists assign numbers or letters to word classes instead of using traditional terminology. In school grammars that follow this practice, Class I words may be loosely equated with traditional nouns, Class II words with verbs, Class III words with adjectives, and Class IV words with adverbs.

Not all structuralists follow this numbering, however. The principal points of difference are (1) whether pronouns constitute a separate class or are a subclass of nouns, and (2) where lines may be drawn between adjectives and adverbs or if, indeed, adjectives and adverbs should not be considered subclasses of a single form class because of the several features that they share.

Most of those writing school grammars have recognized that today's teachers and students find themselves in a period of transition and have adopted structural methods of establishing word classes but have used traditional terminology and category divisions where possible.

Differences among structuralists should not be allowed to obscure the key differences between traditionalists and structuralists generally. These are the differences in methods of definition—traditionalists rely on notional or referential meaning; structuralists on the criteria listed above—and the firm distinction structuralists draw between form class words and function words. These differences are most clearly shown by a consideration of the specific ways in which the structuralist goes about his classification.

FORM CLASS WORDS

Nouns—Class I words

Forms occurring in this class have several distinctive structural characteristics. These characteristics are discussed below.

1. INFLECTIONAL PARADIGM Generally speaking, nouns are forms that will accept inflections for the plural and the possessive. The inflectional paradigm is made up of the base—or singular—form, the plural, the possessive, and the possessive plural forms.

2. DERIVATIONAL PARADIGM Many forms may be recognized as nouns on the basis of various noun-marking derivational suffixes, added either to bound bases or to other words—often words belonging to other form classes. There are literally dozens of these endings. They may be sorted on the basis of the form classes to which they are added in most cases. For example, *-er, -or,* and *-ment* adapt verbs to use as nouns; *-ness* is added to adjectives to produce noun forms and so on.

3. INTONATION PATTERN Differences of stress often separate nouns from verbs as with *ímprint/imprínt, súspèct/sùspéct,* and *cóntràct/còntráct.* Heavier stress on the first syllable almost always signals a noun; heavier stress on the second signals a verb. In larger contexts ambiguity may result without the distinctions supplied by intonation differences. Headlines such as "Union pickets protest meeting," demonstrate these problems.

4. POSITION OR WORD ORDER Nouns fill certain characteristic positions in relation to other parts of speech. The most obvious is that just before a verb. School grammars frequently make use of *test frames,* leaving blanks in simple sentences that may be filled by members of a single form class. It is a most basic type of discovery procedure. A simple set of test frames for the noun might be:

The _____ is here. These _____ are here.

These make use of the function words *the* and *these* and the fact that nouns show plural number in addition to the device of position.

5. FUNCTION WORDS In English noun determiners immediately precede nouns or precede them with certain words in between. Some noun determiners never appear except when followed by a noun and invariably signal its coming. These are the articles *the, a,* and *an* and possessive pronouns *my, your, our,* and *their.* Other pronouns are quite frequently used as determiners but have other functions as well. These are the demonstratives *this, that, these,* and *those* and the other possessive pronouns *his, her,* and *its.*

Pronouns

When considered a separate class, pronouns are Class II words, but since most school texts consider them a subcategory of nouns that practice will be followed here.

In contrast to nouns, pronouns constitute a closed class—no new pronouns have been added to English for hundreds of years. If anything the class has become smaller as few speakers of English now make use of the forms *thee, thou, thy,* and *thine.*

Personal pronouns fall into an inflectional paradigm that is similar to, but not exactly like, that for nouns. Forms show both number and the possessive case but they also show gender and the nominative and objective cases. Positionally, the pronouns are identifiable by the ability of each to substitute for a type of noun. Intonation patterns in these cases are the same or are similar to those for the nouns. Determiners work only with true nouns.

Verbs—Class II words

Forms occurring in this class have several distinctive structural characteristics. These characteristics are discussed below.

1. INFLECTIONAL PARADIGM English verbs commonly have five forms, the base form and four inflected forms. The four verb inflections are the present third person singular, the past, the present participle and the past participle forms. These make up the inflectional paradigm for English verbs. The present third singular is similar in many ways to the noun inflections—another indication of the fact that grammar develops according to complex unconscious forces rather than according to the laws of some preconceived logic! The past tense or preterit is commonly formed with the *-ed* ending, but there are several irregular allomorphs.

The present participle is formed by an -ing suffix. The past participle makes use of -ed and -en endings or internal vowel changes. In a class by itself in many ways is the verb be, which has eight inflected forms.

2. DERIVATIONAL PARADIGM   Some verbs are marked by suffixes such as the -ate ending added to bound bases and nouns, the -ize added to bound bases, nouns and adjectives, and the -fy added to bound bases, nouns and adjectives, and the prefix en- added to nouns and some other verbs.

3. INTONATION PATTERN   See contrasts with nouns marked by intonation.

4. POSITION OR WORD ORDER   Some positions mark verbs and simple test frames may be constructed for these. Verbs commonly occupy the first position in requests, a position between two nouns, or between noun and adjective.

5. FUNCTION WORDS   The function words that work with verbs are the various forms of the auxiliary verbs have and be and the modals can, may, shall, will, must and a few others. These fall into groups marked by their ability to work with the various inflected forms of the verb outlined above.

Adjectives—Class **III** words

Forms occurring in this class have several distinctive structural characteristics. These characteristics are discussed below.

1. INFLECTIONAL PARADIGM   True adjectives commonly show comparative and superlative degrees by adding -er and -est inflections. Derived adjectives make use of the function words more and most for this purpose.

2. DERIVATIONAL PARADIGM   True adjectives fit into derivational patterns with nouns formed by adding the suffix -ness to true adjectives and adverbs formed by adding the suffix -ly to the same adjectives. Examples are: happy-happiness-happily/red-redness-redly/eager-eager-ness-eagerly/quiet-quietness-quietly. Adjectives are derived from other words by adding such endings as -y, ic, and -ous to nouns and bound bases; -ful and -less to nouns; -able, -ent, and -ive to verbs and bound bases.

3. INTONATION PATTERN   Occasionally a noun which is a compound word is distinguished from an adjective-plus-noun by means of differences in intonation. Examples are blàck bóard/bláckbòard, white hoúse/White Hoùse. (The last example is considered by structuralists to be a compound noun even though its written representation has a space between its parts.)

4. POSITION OF WORD ORDER   The most common positions for adjectives are between determiner and noun and after a copulative verb or a qualifier. A test frame that indicates these positions is:

The _____ girl was very _____.

5. FUNCTION WORDS   The function words that work with adjectives also work with some adverbs and cannot, therefore, be called adjective determiners unless adverbs and adjectives are seen as members of a single inclusive class. These function words are called *qualifiers* (or sometimes *intensifiers*) and include the forms *more* and *most* as well as *very, quite, rather, less,* and so on. Occasionally they are used in combination.

Adverbs—Class IV words

Many of the members of the adverb class share several structural distinctions with adjectives. In many cases decisions as to whether a word is an adjective or an adverb must depend upon a combination of structural devices and tests rather than a single one. They are said to have the structural characteristics discussed below.

1. INFLECTIONAL PARADIGM   In a few cases adverbs admit the comparative and superlative degree endings -*er* and -*est* but they usually make use of function words *more* and *most* for this purpose. Some adverbs have a base form that also serves as an adjective. Examples are *fast* and *hard*. Identification of this form class is, therefore, dependent upon other structural devices.

2. DERIVATIONAL PARADIGM   The most common adverb-marking suffix is the -*ly* added to adjectives. A few adverbs are marked by the endings -*ward, -wards* and -*wise* added to nouns. Still another group of adverbs is formed by combining noun determiners *some, any, every,* and *no* with function words *where, way, how,* and *place.*

3. INTONATION PATTERN   The intonation patterns of larger structures often show adverbs patterning closely with verbs in contrast to adjectives which usually pattern with nouns.

4. POSITION OR WORD ORDER   Most adverbs in English are extremely mobile. In some cases a decision as to whether or not a given form is an adverb rests on whether it will move easily from one position to another. Various types may fill any of several positions or positional combinations but almost all can fill the position following a noun-verb-complement sequence as in the test frame:

The boy ate his cookies _____.

Virtually all adverbs may appear in this position with shifts in nouns to allow for lexical differences. Other environments may be found for some types of adverbs but all types fit this one.

FUNCTION WORDS

These words have been defined as those having little or no lexical meaning. They are used in combination with form class words in larger structures. The relationship of function words to form class words is often likened to that of mortar and bricks. Major categories differ very slightly from one structuralist to another. The list below is fairly representative.

DETERMINERS The workings of this class of function words is described in some detail under the form class with which they appear, the nouns, or class I words.

AUXILIARY VERBS Forms of the auxiliaries *have* and *be* work with various inflected forms of verbs, or class II words. Modals are usually considered a subcategory since their operation is somewhat different from that of *have* and *be*.

QUALIFIERS These forms work with both adjectives and adverbs. Some of the most frequently used are listed under consideration of those two form classes.

PREPOSITIONS These forms introduce modifying or qualifying phrases set apart by intonation pattern and the presence of the preposition form.

CONJUNCTIONS These forms always work as coordinators of linguistic forms or syntactic units having equal value.

SUBORDINATORS These forms connect dependent clauses and include words like *because, after, although, unless,* and so on, as well as the relative pronouns *who, whose, which,* and *that.*

INTERROGATIVES These forms operate in the formation of questions and include words like *when, where, why, how,* and so on, as well as the interrogative pronouns *who, which,* and *what.*

Some words perform such distinctive linguistic service that they are, quite literally, in a class by themselves. Among these are *please, yes, no, not* and the so-called "temporary subject" *there* as in "There's a man out there."

The form classes and the function word categories may be subdivided for more precise definition of their syntactic operation. Here there may be still other differences between structuralists.

The groups of form class words may be designated by their traditional titles—noun, verb, adjective, and adverb—or they may be numbered form classes 1, 2, 3, and 4 or I, II, III, and IV. Each group may be further subdivided and the resulting groups may be assigned different names or designations. For example, some may refer to *base adjectives* and *derived adjectives* while others may speak of *adjectives* and *adjectivals*. This kind of difference is not whim or perversity; the categories are set up in slightly different ways by each grammarian and each feels the need to make it very clear that his categories are not precisely the same as those set up by someone else.

Each is attempting to describe highly complex systems-within-systems and each hopes to do so as concisely and clearly as possible. While the grammatical system of English is, generally speaking, very orderly, there are idiomatic quirks in the language that defy any rules to categorize them neatly. For example, there is the reluctance of English speakers to form a plural of the word *music*. They use, instead, the term "pieces of music" when a plural is virtually demanded by syntactic context. On the other hand there are terms that appear to be plurals—they end in *-s* and have dual-appearing referents—such as *pants, scissors,* and *pliers* that English speakers flatly refuse to treat as singular terms. These terms apparently have no singular form and when a singular form is demanded by syntactic context, the English speaker gets around the problem by saying "a pair of. . . ."

In order to be true to the objectives he had set for himself—describing the language as it is used by speakers of the language—the structuralist must cope with such matters as precisely as possible while, at the same time, keeping his description from becoming any more complex and unwieldy than absolutely necessary. That each may, as a result, try slightly different means of description is not at all surprising.

These differences in detail should not be allowed to obscure the fact that, fundamentally, the structural grammarians agree—to a man—on their general approach to the problem of analyzing the grammar of the English language. This approach recognizes the primacy of speech and the need to begin with a phonological and morphological analysis of the language. It recognizes the fundamental difference between form class words and function words. It recognizes the criteria of inflection, derivational contrast, intonation patterns, position or word order and the use of function words for identifying the form class words.

When function words are subdivided, some structuralists assign a letter to each group, A, B, C, D, and so on. Others assign each group its traditional name where possible and names denoting the functions of the words in the groups to others. The initials of these names may then be assigned to groups, as D for determiners, A for auxiliary, P for preposition, and so on. Again, these are differences in detail. Structural grammarians as a group agree that function words have little or no lexical meaning other than the grammatical relationships they communicate in combination with other forms. They agree to an overwhelming degree on the criteria for establishing the groupings of these words. These criteria are position, intonation pattern, and the functions of the words in phrases, clauses, and sentences.

SYNTACTIC COMBINATIONS

When smaller structures enter into combinations, some consideration must be given to the relationships holding between them within the combination. For example, "Birds fly" consists of structures commonly called *noun* and *verb*. The combination is a larger structure called a *sentence*. Within the sentence, *birds* is both a noun and the *subject* of the sentence. The designation *noun* identifies it as a *structure;* the designation *subject* identifies the *function* it performs in combination with the verb. *Fly* is identified as a *structure* called a *verb* which fulfills the *function* of *predicate* in the sentence. Analysis of any larger structure involves sorting its parts into types of smaller structures and identifying the functions performed in the combination.

Structural grammarians vary somewhat in the methods used to analyze complex grammatical structures in English. Three of the principal methodologies will be touched upon here.

Phrase analysis

One means of dealing with these problems begins with consideration of word "clusters" that are set apart on the basis of the intonation pattern that they show. A group of words appearing between well-defined junctures is described as a *phrase* or *cluster*. In general, these phrases function as units in larger structures and they fall into groups based on the type of function the *unit* performs. Noun phrases or clusters, verb phrases or clusters and various types of modifying or qualifying phrases—adjectival, adverbial, prepositional, and so on—may be defined. Analysis may then be made of relationships holding between the various types when they appear in various combinations. Finally, clause and sentence types may be defined.

Immediate constituent analysis

A second method—and perhaps the most widely used means of dealing with the problems of English syntax—is immediate constituent analysis, commonly called IC analysis.

In IC analysis, sentences are divided into their principal parts or immediate constituents, each of these is again divided and subdivided until the ultimate constituents of the sentence are reached. For example:

> 1. *The boys / shyly touched the puppy.*
>   *shyly touched / the puppy.*
>   *The / boys / shyly / touched / the / puppy.*
> 2. *Small puppies   /   are fat and frisky.*
>   *are / fat and frisky.*
>   *Small / puppies / are / fat / and / frisky.*

Further cuts might even divide the plural morphemes from *boy* and *puppy,* the inflectional *-ed* from *touch,* and the *-ly* from *shy.* In the interest of simplicity, we will concern ourselves only with those cuts shown above.

Relationships holding between the ICs may be analyzed and identified after each cut is made. In the first example sentence, the first cut yields structures that function as subject and predicate:

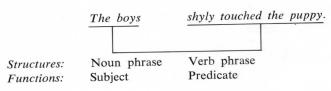

	The boys	shyly touched the puppy.
Structures:	Noun phrase	Verb phrase
Functions:	Subject	Predicate

The second cut yields structures that function as verbal element and complement (or object) within the predicate:

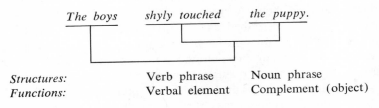

	The boys	shyly touched	the puppy.
Structures:		Verb phrase	Noun phrase
Functions:		Verbal element	Complement (object)

The final cuts yield:

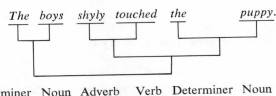

	The	boys	shyly	touched	the	puppy.
Structures:	Determiner	Noun	Adverb	Verb	Determiner	Noun
Functions:	Modifier	Head	Modifier	Head	Modifier	Head

Among other things, this type of analysis gives rise to the practice of referring to *noun-headed structures* and *verb-headed structures* when speaking of clusters or phrases where the construction is one of modification. Again the adjectives and adverbs show similarities in syntactic function. The relationships holding between the determiners and nouns above are the same as that holding between the adverb and verb.

In the second example sentence, the first cut yields structures that function as subject and predicate:

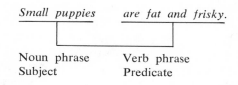

Structures:	Noun phrase	Verb phrase
Functions:	Subject	Predicate

The second cut yields:

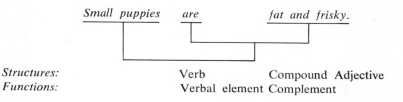

Structures:		Verb	Compound Adjective
Functions:		Verbal element	Complement

The final cuts yield one structure composed of head and modifier and another composed of two coordinates joined by the conjunction *and* serving as connector:

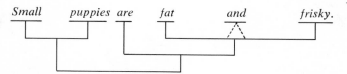

Structures:	Adjective	Noun	Verb	Adjective	Conjunction	Adjective
Functions:	Modifier	Head	Verbal	Coordinate	Connector	Coordinate

IC analysis has two important points in its favor as far as classroom use is concerned. First, the layers of relationships in English sentences is graphically displayed. English syntax is based on this ability of structures to function within larger structures, which are, in turn, serving other functions in still larger, more complex structures.

Diagraming a more complex sentence such as:

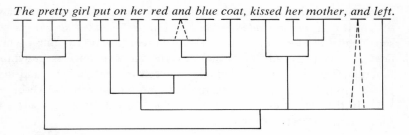

The pretty girl put on her red and blue coat, kissed her mother, and left.

demonstrates the nature of the relationships that must be negotiated if a hearer or reader is to understand such a sentence. However complex the diagram may appear, it is apparent that the complex nature of the relationships is in the sentence as well as in the diagram. Anyone who is capable of understanding the meaning of the sentence obviously has the mental capacity to keep all those relationships afloat as he hears or reads the sentence.

A second very real advantage to such a method of analysis and diagraming is that the word order is not disturbed in any way. This advantage is best demonstrated by sorting the relationships found in three sentences which are composed of the same words but which are different in their word order.

1. *The boy played marbles on his knees.*

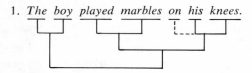

2. *The boy on his knees played marbles.*

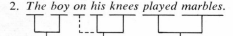

3. *On his knees the boy played marbles.*

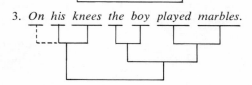

These sentences may be said to be stylistically different. In the first, the prepositional phrase *on his knees* modifies the verb phrase; in the second, it modifies the noun phrase; in the third, it modifies all of the rest of the sentence.

Although there are many methods of traditional diagraming, most would be likely to diagram all three sentences above in exactly the same way:

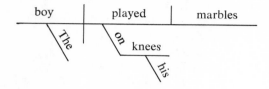

Such diagraming not only ignores the word order of the three sentences, it distorts the meaning of sentences two and three where the modification operates in distinctive ways.

One drawback must be noted with regard to immediate constituent diagraming. This drawback is found in the need to connect discontinuous elements in sentences such as the question below.

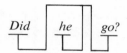

Even so, there is little to prefer in traditional diagraming of such sentences. Traditional diagraming usually dismembers questions like the one above, turning them into statements—a practice which reveals little about how the syntactic relationships in English questions actually operate.

Sentence formulas

A third means of dealing with the problems of English syntax is one that begins with a consideration of basic sentence patterns and proceeds to analyze the relationships between the different parts of the patterns. Each of the parts of very simple sentences can be expanded in various ways so that more complex sentence patterns—and more complex layers of relationships—are produced.

Sentence patterns of the simplest noun-verb, noun-verb-noun, noun-verb-adjective types are considered first. The sentence parts are designated by the numbers and letters assigned to their form class or function word groups. A short sample list might be:

Form Class Words	*Function Words*
1 noun or pronoun	D determiner
2 verb	A auxiliary
3 adjective	Q qualifier
4 adverb	P preposition

Simple sentence types and some variations on each type might then include the following:

Sentence Type I	Variations
1 — 2	D — 1 — 2
	D — 3 — 1 — 2
	D — 1 — 2 — 4
	D — Q — 3 — 1 — 2

Sentence Type II	Variations
1 — 2 — 3	D — 1 — 2 — 3
	D — 3 — 1 — 2 — 3
	D — 1 — 2 — Q — 3
	D — 3 — 1 — 2 — Q — 3

Sentence Type III	Variations
1 — 2 — 1	D — 1 — 2 — 1
	D — 1 — P — D — 1 — 2 — 1
	D — 1 — 2 — 1 — P — D — 1
	1 — P — D — 1 — 4 — 2 — D — 1

Sentence Type IV	Variations
1 — 2 — 1 — 1	1 — 2 — D — 1 — D — 1
	D — 1 — Q — 4 — 2 — D — 1 — 1
	D — 3 — 2 — 1 — D — 3 — 2
	1 — 2 — D — 1 — D — 1 — 4

These patterns can be used quite effectively for classroom exercises in which students make vocabulary substitutions for the numbers and letters of the formulas. The formulas can be expanded for more and more complex noun and verb clusters with prepositional phrases, subordinate clauses, structures of coordination, and so on.

PART THREE

VARIETIES OF
AMERICAN ENGLISH

9

DIALECT AND USAGE

Most of the objection to structural linguistic methods of describing the grammar of the English language falls into three major areas. Those who prefer the prescriptive rules of traditional school grammars maintain that

1. The separation of grammar and semantics is an artificial one.

2. The tremendous variety of syntactic patterns possible in English present far greater complexities for analysis than those presented by the sound system or even the morphological system, and the methods of structural linguistics have not even approached an acceptable description of the rich syntactic complexity of the English language.

3. The indiscriminate gathering of data practiced by structuralists destroys any basis for distinguishing between effective, efficient language habits and those that are apt to produce lack of precision and, therefore, misunderstanding among users of the language. Linguistic anarchy may be free of authoritarian value judgments, but it is also apt to be short on commonly held principles which allow for the effective communication of ideas and experience that is the primary purpose of language.

The first two of these objections are matters of basic philosophy and method; the third is based, at least in part, on misunderstanding which may be clarified by looking into the structuralist position on matters of dialect and usage.

So much has been written about dialect and usage in recent years that the meanings of the terms themselves have become somewhat blurred. Some writers refer to the standard dialect, others to standard usage, and still others avoid the problem by referring to something called "Standard English." Both dialect and usage refer to differences in language habits and practices among groups of people speaking the same language.

For the linguist, *dialect* means all the language habits—pronunciation, vocabulary, and syntactic combination—which distinguish one regional or social variety of a language from another. A dialect may be determined on the basis of geographic areas, social distinctions, or both.

Usage usually refers to language choices with particular emphasis on specific items of pronunciation, vocabulary, or syntactic combination and, frequently, the establishment of standards of correctness or appropriateness. Correct usage is to language what rules of etiquette are to human behavior.

Those interested in studying dialect and usage differences set a variety of objectives for themselves, go about their research and analysis in a variety of ways, and arrive at a startling array of results.

To understand and evaluate any book or article on dialect or usage, the reader should take careful note of several key points:

1.   What were the writer's objectives?

2.   How were lists of test items established?

3.   How were judges, informants, or source materials selected?

4.   How were the sources grouped? For example, what was the basis for dividing the informants or written sources into geographic or social areas?

5.   How much data was gathered?

6.   How was the data tabulated and analyzed?

Researchers investigating the varieties of American English have set a number of different objectives for themselves. The major areas of emphasis have been (1) dialect geography, which deals with the different varieties of English to be found in various parts of the country; (2) the study of social dialects, which deals with differences found among groups of speakers set apart by differences in educational background, economic situation, and social prestige of one kind or another; and (3) studies aimed at defining that most elusive of language varieties, Standard American English.

DIALECT GEOGRAPHY

In matters of dialect, as in many other areas of language study, the paths of the linguistic scholar and the teacher of English have often taken different directions. For many years, while school textbook writers and teachers conformed to the prescriptions of authority, linguists were fascinated by the fact that dialect differences did exist and were interested in comparing and contrasting them. Linguists had no desire to pin "good" and "bad"—or even "preferred" and "disapproved"—labels on any dialect. They gathered information, as they always had, for no other purpose than to sort and analyze and study it.

In the early part of this century, several American linguists were most interested in the findings of European dialect geographers who had been mapping dialect differences in Germany, France, England, and other countries for nearly a hundred years. After a decade of attempting to institute some comprehensive study of the differences in the speech habits of Americans, definite action was at last taken in 1929. Proposals for an American Linguistic Atlas were pending before both the Modern Language Association of America and the American Council of Learned Societies. At a meeting of representatives from both groups, financed by the National Council of Teachers of English, details for the proposed study were put into concrete form. Funds were allocated for a pilot project confined to the New England states.

With European experts in linguistic geography as consultants, American linguists worked out a design for their project. Primary concerns for those in charge of the field research were (1) methods of selection and classification of sample communities; (2) choices of individual informants; (3) methods to be used for interviewing and for recording the information given by informants; and (4) the selection of items of pronunciation, vocabulary and syntax which would, when surveyed and compared, produce the most reliable index to the speech habits of those who lived in the areas studied.

Painstaking attention to detail marked this project and those which were to follow. Actual gathering of data for *The Linguistic Atlas of New England* began in 1931, and the completed work was published in 1939–1943. Similar studies have been made of the Atlantic states except for Florida, the North Central states of Wisconsin, Michigan, Illinois, Indiana, Kentucky, and Ohio, the Upper Midwestern states of Minnesota, Iowa, North and South Dakota, and Nebraska, and several other, smaller areas of the country, including Colorado and New Mexico and parts of Texas, Tennessee, Louisiana, and the Pacific Coast states.

Exhaustive analysis of the data gathered for these studies exploded much of the myth and misconception about the speech habits of Americans. Instead of the North-South-Western areas that had been generally accepted as accounting for any differences in the ways that Americans used their language, *The Linguistic Atlas* maps showed two heavy east-west dividing lines separating the eastern part of the United States into Northern, Midland, and Southern dialect areas. Later studies showed that these areas had a tendency to follow the population moves of westward expansion with interesting patterns of mixture showing west of the Mississippi River. Subdivisions of the major areas reflected the settlement of large numbers of people of similar national origin, natural barriers to population movement and other nonlinguistic factors.

Dialect geographers found that the most clearly defined differences in regional dialects were concentrated primarily in the areas of (1) pronunciation, particularly in the matter of vowel sounds; (2) vocabulary; and (3) verb forms, particularly in choices of past and past participle forms of irregular verbs. The dialect boundaries established by phonological comparison were reinforced by those marking differences in choices of vocabulary items and reinforced again by those marking differences in choices of verb forms.

The language habits of the American people could no longer be dumped into two large bins marked "good" and "bad" with a few quirks of New England and Southern pronunciations shrugged off as insignificant localisms. For one thing, some speech habits recognized as perfectly acceptable by the cultured, well-educated people in the North were frowned upon by Midland purists and both groups accepted other habits which grated on the ears of Southern aristocrats. Some Southern habits might claim greater similarity to British ways of using the language and still elicit cool rejection from Northern purists.

Like many other worthwhile research projects, *The Linguistic Atlas* studies raised as many questions as they answered.

SOCIAL DIALECTS

The informants whose speech habits were recorded by *The Linguistic Atlas* field workers had been chosen primarily on the basis of geographic location but other criteria were also brought to bear in their selection. Informants in each geographic area were chosen and classified on the basis of age, education, social, and economic differences. Three broad categories were established. Type I informants were elderly, native-born residents in each community who, because of considerations of education, profession, and social distinctions, might represent earlier regional dialect patterns; type II informants were middle-aged natives of each community with high school or equivalent education; and type III informants were cultured, college-educated members of larger communities.

This recognition of the differences in the language habits of socially different groups of people was not a revolutionary new idea. Learning the speech habits of those who have greater social, economic, and educational prestige has long been recognized as one of the prerequisites for upward social mobility. Dialect geographers gathered a steadily mounting body of evidence as to the nature and extent of these differences. Their findings led several dialect researchers to concentrate their efforts more specifically on the study of social dialects.

Methods of defining socially different groups of speakers were refined. Most studies of social dialect distinctions were confined to a single geographic area. The populations of such large cities as New York; Washington, D.C.; and Detroit were subjects of several of the more rigidly controlled and exhaustively analyzed surveys. The masses of evidence gathered by social dialect researchers gave statistical strength to several rather broad generalizations about social dialects.

First, differences in the language habits of socially different speakers were not random "mistakes"; dialects spoken by those groups set apart by social, economic, and educational deprivation were as *systematic* as prestige dialects. Second, speakers of different social dialects showed a remarkable ability to evaluate the social position of speakers of dialects other than their own. Third, speakers of nonstandard dialects often showed a markedly defensive attitude with regard to their own dialect.

Each of these points had important implications for teachers of English.

Working with the evidence showing that nonstandard dialects were both systematically different from the standard dialect and often quite consistent in their differences, many teachers saw an opportunity to devise better teaching methods for dealing with students who spoke nonstandard dialects. For example, American Negro dialects show a number of systematic variations on the standard. A few of these differences are:

1. In the pronunciation of consonant clusters such as those found in the words *asks, dentists,* and *facts.*

2. The dropping of final -*r* in such words as *door, four,* and *floor.*

3. Consistent use of the plural -*s,* even with words having plurals based on internal vowel change, resulting in "double plurals" such as *mens* and *childrens.*

4. Leveling of the present third singular verb endings resulting in *he talk, she try,* and so on.

5. Substitution of past participle forms for past tense forms of verbs resulting in *I seen, she taken,* and so on.

Using complete lists of such differences as guides for lesson plans suggested teaching methods far superior to former practices of random corrections which had accomplished little beyond alienating students from their English teachers and from standard English as well. These methods, similar in many ways to improved methods of teaching English as a foreign language, involve approaching the problems of teaching a new dialect in much the same way that teachers approach the problems of teaching any new language. Using a knowledge of the language habits that the student already has as a basis for comparison with those to be taught, broad areas of differences in sound, vocabulary, basic grammatical and syntactic patterns can be dealt with on a step-by-step basis. No teacher would attempt to teach English to a class of French-speaking students without having some knowledge of both languages. Teaching a prestige dialect of English as a foreign language is taught requires that teachers have some knowledge of the dialect that their students already speak as well as a thorough knowledge of the prestige dialect.

A second point of profound interest to teachers was the fact that speakers of nonstandard dialects who did not seem to be aware of their own language habits were apparently quite capable of evaluating the social standing of other speakers on the basis of their language habits. Many teachers believed that this ability could be put to productive use in the classroom. Tape recorders and the language lab techniques of foreign language instruction have been introduced into many English classrooms where the students are speakers of nonstandard dialects.

Finally, teachers who studied the results of social dialect research began to develop new attitudes toward the native dialects of their students. Speakers of nonstandard dialects have understandably strong emotional ties to their own speech habits. These speech patterns are, quite literally, a fundamental part of the speaker's personality. To ask that an individual completely obliterate so great a part of himself is setting too great a price on a passport to economic and educational acceptance. Such demands insist that a student cut bridges to his past, to emotional security and familiar surroundings in order to build bridges to an unfamiliar and unknown future.

Educators who hope to help young people to greater educational, economic, and social opportunity have come to realize that they cannot force their students to obliterate their familiar language habits any more than foreign language teachers can force their students to renounce forever their use of the English language. Instead, teachers have begun to refocus their efforts toward giving such students a command of standard English *in addition to* the dialect that they already know. Instead of demanding that a student trade the dialect of home, family and his own identity for the language of the market place, teachers can bend their efforts toward a much more humanitarian—and realistic—goal: helping their students to become *bidialectal* as foreign language teachers help their students to become bilingual.

SETTING STANDARDS OF USAGE

Until the 1930s, those who wrote on the subject of standard English usage were almost invariably interested in authoritative judgment. A single writer might offer his personal opinion on the acceptability of each item in question and state his reasons for each of his decisions. These decisions were usually based on historical precedent, the usage of certain recognized authors, etymology, analogy, or logic. Many of these decisions varied from one authority to another. Because of the complex history of the English language, a variety of decisions on any one usage could be "proven." Other writers submitted lists of items to a panel or jury of eminent authorities and tabulated the voting. In both cases the objective was not to discover the ways that groups of speakers used the language but to discover how authorities felt all speakers of the language *ought to* use it. If, for example, authorities decreed that English speakers must never say *back of* or *in back of* rather than *behind,* then writers of textbooks, English teachers and editors felt it their duty to blot out the use of *back of* and *in back of* by whatever means at their disposal.

Developments in descriptive linguistic method and dialect research in the past few decades have placed the arguments about preferred versus rejected English usage in a new arena. Most of those seeking to establish standards of usage recognize that their efforts can no longer seek acceptance on the often disputed grounds of etymology, "logic," analogy with Latin, or historical precedent. Instead, choices among various pronunciations, vocabulary items, verb forms, and syntactic combinations are more and more frequently based on evidence as to which choices are habitually made by certain respected users of the language. Preferred usages are, quite simply, value judgments. Like other value judgments, they are based on complex cultural factors.

Because of the complexity of these social and cultural factors, few, if any, arbiters of usage still insist on a single standard of correctness. Instead shades of correctness, called *levels* or *varieties of usage,* are determined according to the means of communication—whether written or spoken—and the purposes to which language is put and the contexts in which it occurs.

There have been many attempts to organize these criteria so that orderly categories may be established. A virtual terminology explosion has brought at least as much heat as light to the subject. Levels or varieties of usage have been variously labeled scientific, literary, formal, standard, general, informal, popular, familiar, colloquial, public, private, substandard, nonstandard, vulgate, and so on and on.

In fairness to those who attempt to define the usage levels of modern speakers of English, it must be noted that clearly defined borderlines between these levels are nonexistent no matter what basis is used for sorting groups of users or language situations. Groups blend into one another like the colors of a natural rainbow.

Here, in outline form, are some of the factors influencing linguistic choice among speakers of English that modern usage experts may or may not take into account.

    I. User of the language
      A. Age
      B. Education
      C. Place of residence
      D. Prestige in the community
      E. Ethnic background

   II. Means of Communication
      A. Spoken
      B. Written

  III. Context
      A. Private
      B. Public

  IV. Special purpose
      A. Scientific
      B. Literary
      C. Ritual, that is, legal, religious
      D. Limited interest groups
        1. Professional
        2. Hobby groups
        3. Sports
        4. Others

This list is not definitive but is presented only to show, as graphically as possible, the complexity of the problems of defining varieties of usage. When all these details are accounted for, there are as many ways of using a language as there are speakers of the language. Furthermore, individuals differ in the ways that they use their language from one period of their lives to another, and in the ways that they use their language in different situations.

Recognition of all the possible shades and levels of usage suggested here is not to say that it is hopeless or useless to attempt to identify the varieties of English in some orderly way. Some order can be brought to a description of varieties of English usage by delimiting objectives. If, for example, we seek to establish a standard usage common to most of the people most of the time, usages particular to such limited groups as professional musicians, baseball players, teen-agers, orchid-growers, and race-horse enthusiasts can be set aside for specialized study along with the peculiarities that result when patterns and pronunciations of other languages are carried over into English by those who learn English as a second language. We may set aside the fading fashions of usage that still find favor among older speakers of the language, and the rigidly fixed language patterns of scientific reports and legal documents, and so on. In the same way we can leave the peculiarities of local dialects to the dialect geographers and broaden our definition of the term "speech community" to include all American speakers of English.

Those factors that remain are those affecting the speech habits of most of the American people most of the time. Our reduced list now looks something like this:

    I. User of the language
      A. Education
      B. Prestige in the community

    II. Means of communication
      A. Spoken
      B. Written

    III. Context
      A. Private
      B. Public

Comparing recordings of the speech of any individual with samples of his written speech will reveal differences in usage choices. Spoken language is fleeting and not susceptible to close scrutiny. Any misunderstanding can usually be seen in the reaction of the hearer and immediately clarified. These things are not true of written language and the usages chosen for written language are, therefore, subject to greater care and consideration.

The speech patterns of any individual are also likely to vary depending on whether he is speaking or writing to a close friend or relative or to someone that he would like to impress with his intelligence and good taste. In the same way that the dress or manners of a single individual vary to suit the situation or surroundings in which he finds himself, so his usage choices are subject to variation. Choices in dress, manners, and language are more relaxed and informal in private, more carefully controlled, even formal, in public.

Listed according to the increasing amount of judgment and precision expended on deliberation and choice by a user of the language, the varieties of usage common to most individuals are:

1. Informal Spoken
2. Informal Written
3. Formal Spoken
4. Formal Written

These four major classifications of language "manners" are common to all literate users of English. But these categories are not sufficient basis for a precise definition of Standard American English. The choices made by some users of the language for informal speaking situations are often strikingly different from those made by others in similar situations. The same can be said for each of the other three situations.

In order to make final choices among these differences, usage experts, like people generally, make judgments based on the prestige and accomplishments of the users of the language. Usage choices made by those who command the respect of others share in that respect. Usage, it has been said, is known by the company it keeps.

Varieties of usage that command respect are facts of life in every complex society. The musical comedy *My Fair Lady* has been translated into most of the languages of Europe with both Eliza Doolittle's Cockney and Henry Higgins' impeccable Standard British English finding counterparts in French, German, Spanish, and all the others. There is also a Japanese version of the play and even one in Russian, in spite of the fact that social class distinctions were, theoretically, wiped out in Russia over fifty years ago. Like standards of conduct and dress, tastes in music, art and even food, these linguistic value judgments are quite real. They may shift and change with time, but they will not disappear.

The standard dialect of American English, or standard usage is then ultimately a value judgment based on

1. The social prestige and accomplishments of certain users of the language.
2. Whether the context is public or private.
3. Whether the medium of communication is spoken or written.

Greatest value is accorded the more carefully considered formal written usage of socially respected members of the speech community. All such judgments are based on generalizations. As in any field of study, some generalizations in matters of language are more reliable than others. Some are little more than personal opinion; others are based on painstaking research and the sifting of enormous amounts of data.

The most widely-accepted works on the usage of Modern American English are based on careful examination of usages appearing in written—usually published—materials prepared by influential, respected American leaders in literature, public affairs, education, business, and journalism. Usage researchers note both the most frequently used forms and constructions and those variants that occur with any degree of frequency.

Authority based on historical precedent, systems of logic, analogy, and etymology has thus been replaced by the pragmatic authority of the most respected users of the language. Traditionalists may still dispute the wisdom of such a replacement but they cannot claim that structural linguistics has destroyed all basis for selection among language habits.

PART FOUR

TRANSFORMATIONAL-
GENERATIVE GRAMMAR

10

GENERATIVE GRAMMAR THEORY

A return to the analogy of linguistic scholar as research scientist and of classroom teacher as family doctor is probably the best way to become reoriented for still another approach to the problem of analyzing the grammar of the English language.

The problems of classroom teachers remain largely the same. What is here that may be useful in helping their students to a more effective and more efficient use of their language skills? It is not necessary that the teacher know every detail of research procedure in order to use the results of the scholar's work—any more than that the doctor know every detail of a research project in order to use a new drug in the treatment of a patient. It is, however, absolutely necessary that the teacher have a working knowledge of the scholar's objectives, procedures and results in order to make use of the scholar's findings in the classroom—just as the doctor must know what disease the medical research scientist's drug is meant to treat, what tests have been made with it, and what the results of those tests are before he prescribes the drug for any of his patients.

Those scholars who study language, whether they be of traditional, structural, or generative persuasion, are dealing with the communicative process. It was suggested at the outset that we consider the communicative process to be made up of the following steps:

1. An ideational stimulus to the mind of the speaker.
2. The formulation of a language statement by the speaker.
3. The physical act of speaking.
4. Sound waves in the atmosphere.

5. The physical process of hearing.
6. The mental sorting of the language statement by hearer.
7. Understanding of the idea by the hearer.

Traditional approaches to grammatical analysis concentrate on the first two steps above. They deal with logical concepts and logical relationships of grammatical forms. If their definitions are sometimes circular, this is not surprising, since they attempt to define words with other words and their definitions of grammatical relationships are framed in statements made up of those relationships. Within the established limitations of their system of logic, it is possible to judge whether the formulation of a language statement is correct or incorrect. Their reliance upon samples of written language—primarily from literary works—for purposes of analysis is quite consistent with this view, for the best-educated people among those using a given language are likely to be those who are best trained to the system of logic within which the grammarians operate. Education of the young then becomes a matter of initiating the student into the accepted system of logic. This initiation is what traditional grammarians have been attempting for many generations. The principal problem has been one of assuming that what is logical in the workings of one language—classical Latin, for example —is logical for all languages, and, therefore, for English. Their failure to recognize the unique logic or system of English grammar is the argument most frequently used against their methods.

As far as the structural grammarians are concerned, English has its own system. In order to discover that system, one must study English. In order to study English according to strict scientific method —which requires observable data—the only steps of the communicative process that are admissible to study are steps three, four, and five above. The emphasis is placed on steps three and four because these are the steps for which the most reliable means of measurement are to be found. With this as their orientation, it is quite understandable that the structuralists do, as we have seen, begin with the smallest units of sound that appear to signal differences in a language, and proceed to ever more complex combinations and systems of using those sounds. The systems they can observe and sort are the logic of the language in question.

Those structuralists who have strong anthropological leanings maintain that steps one and two occur almost simultaneously, or that they are virtually a single step. The same may be said for steps six and seven. They point out that in even the shortest exchanges of communication, there are the unmeasurable factors of the psychology of the participants, the social and immediate contexts, and "feedback." For example, a child may say to his mother, "There's a unicorn outside my window." Steps one through six may be said to operate perfectly, but the mother does not immediately rush to the window to view the unicorn, nor does she hysterically call in the psychoanalyst for her child. Clearly, other factors, in addition to the grammar of English, are operating.

The structuralist, then, sets his limitations at the boundaries of that which is measurable and leaves the rest to those who work in other disciplines and have their own methodologies. Definition of the Standard Dialect is a value judgment that he undertakes only with the stipulation that this involves arbitrarily set social and economic levels and limitations of age and education for those whose language is considered Standard.

The structuralist recognizes the fact that English is an extremely flexible and adaptable language, even though he works with a comparatively limited corpus of material. Fries' 250,000-word corpus of recorded telephone conversations is impressive, but it becomes almost miscroscopic if consideration is given to what might have been garnered if similar recordings had been made in all the cities of the world where English is spoken instead of only in a part of Ann Arbor, Michigan. In order to approach a thoroughgoing analysis of the structures possible in English, the structuralist must rely on his own intuition and invent phrases and sentences that would be acceptable to him under certain circumstances. A truly exhaustive survey of possibilities, as far as syntax is concerned, is a difficult, if not impossible objective.

Generalizations can be made on the basis of samples. No one, however, can ever hope to record all the variables of a living human language. Edward Sapir's frequently quoted remark that "all grammars leak" is not so much an indictment of grammarians as it is a recognition of the immensity—the virtual impossibility—of the task of sorting the complexity of living language into tidy little boxes.

The generative grammarian establishes his objectives and his limitations in other ways—ways that cause great misgivings among those concerned with strict scientific method. In order to appreciate his reasons for setting his objectives and limitations as he does, consideration must be given to those facts which he emphasizes to a far greater degree than does the structuralist.

The generative grammarian argues that the speaker and hearer of English have a vast common ground in steps two and six of the communicative process. If this were not so, communication between them would be impossible. Formulation of language statements to be spoken or written, and the sorting of those that are heard or read must be based on the same basic code. He contends that a vast catalog of sentences might be established after the analysis of enormous quantities of material and still the list would be woefully incomplete. Even the establishment of sentence patterns and their possible variations could continue to the limits of the absurd. Is there not, he asks, a better, more concise method of dealing with the complexity and creativity of the English language? Is there a way to "crack the code" that speakers of English share in order to negotiate steps two and six of the communicative process—even though the speakers and hearers deal with new and, in many cases, unique sentences every day of their lives?

Structuralists contend that the generative grammarian, in exploring areas other than those where data may be objectively verified, has stepped beyond the acceptable limitations of linguistic investigation. But the generative grammarian argues that the ability of speakers of a language to formulate, and their hearers to comprehend utterances they have never heard before is undeniably a fact—and one that is of vital interest to the linguistic researcher.

Another fact that fascinates the generative grammarian is that children are able to acquire a high degree of facility with the grammatical system of their language at an extremely early age. Children who are still in diapers begin to verbalize. They point to things and repeat the words adults say to them: "Mama," "doggy," "cup." Incredibly soon they are able to think in abstract terms. A two-year-old's mother may say "That's a no-no," and the child knows that she is not giving a name to an object. The term "no-no" may have been applied within the hour to a bowl of flowers, a lighted cigarette, a piece of bric-a-brac, and another child's toy. The mother means "That may hurt you; it may break; I may punish you for touching it," or any combination of these. And a child of two knows what she means. Steps one through six have been successfully negotiated. Other factors may influence step seven, and the child may test the mother's statement, but that is a matter for the child psychologist or the psycholinguist to ponder.

Soon other evidence of the child's ability to grasp his language tools and use them becomes apparent. The child's father says, "Go ask your mother where she put the hammer." The child goes to his mother and says, "Daddy wants the hammer." He has created a sentence—one that he probably has never heard before but one that adheres to the rules of his language—in spite of the fact that no one has ever mentioned to him that the language *has* rules, let alone what those rules are.

A child may be said to perform two language learning operations. While he is learning differences in meaning (that is, some small furry animals are *dogs,* some are *cats,* others are *squirrels,* and so on), he is also learning to put words together in grammatical patterns (that is, *the top of my head,* not **my head top;* *fire burns,* not **fire of burn,* and so on). He learns, in short, both *semantic definition* and *grammatical rule.*

A child learns the language or languages spoken around him. The process begins almost at once. The speech heard by an infant is almost never ordered to aid him in learning grammatical patterns. It may, indeed, be highly erratic, as in the case of the parent who insists on speaking "baby talk" to the child. Another child may be exposed to two entirely different systems at the same time, as in the case of the bilingual home, and, incidentally, learn both systems!

Most vocabulary items are patiently repeated to a child until he learns them; he relies on this specific instruction. But the grammar of his language is another matter. He learns the highly complex patterns of putting his words together without specific instruction. He does not know that he is learning rules of grammar when he begins to put phrases and sentences together. He learns to comprehend the sentences of others, he learns to create sentences of his own, without knowing how he knows. This is the *intuitive* knowledge that generative grammarians attempt to describe.

Most children are intuitively in control of a substantial part of the grammar of their language by the time they are four or five. A child of six is expected to have a command of the grammatical system of English sufficient to allow him to enter school and consider hundreds, even thousands, of new sentences every day. His command of the system even enables him to consider and assimilate whole new concepts when they are presented within the framework of the system. This is not a system of logic that he must be taught but one that he possesses.

If this is the case, teachers ask at this point, why do we need to teach the child any grammar? If he already knows the grammar of his language, what is left to teach him?

There are at least two very good answers to these questions. First, in the case of the student who comes from an environment where the Standard Dialect is spoken, there is the fascination of seeing, in precise terms, an analysis of what he is doing when he uses his language. An awareness of the system in these terms allows him still greater conscious control of the sentences that he generates. A person who plays a musical instrument "by ear" may be able to produce lovely and enjoyable music. However, his ability will not be harmed but will, in fact, be enhanced by instruction in harmonics, musicology, and musical notation. Such training should help him bring conscious control to his natural skills.

The student whose dialect is different in some ways from the Standard needs to be shown where those differences are as simply and concisely as possible. If he can be shown that his usage is systematic and that the Standard is systematic but that there are differences in the systems, then he finds himself in a situation that is similar to that of a native speaker of English confronted with the task of learning a foreign language. The rules he learns apply to the sentences he will create in the future; he is not simply confronted with isolated corrections of what is "wrong" with what he has already said.

The generative grammarian cites the manifestations of the innate language acquiring abilities of the human mind. Young children learn the grammar of their language in ways that seem almost miraculous considering the erratic data that is "programmed into" their brains. There is evidence that this ability must be stimulated at an early age. Studies of children who grew up with little or no human companionship —psychologists refer to them as *feral* children—indicate a permanent crippling of their ability to acquire the use of any language beyond animal sounds. If early stimulation is not present, the innate language-acquiring ability apparently atrophies. There is also overwhelming evidence to indicate that a child's ability to acquire a second language is at its peak during his first ten or twelve years. Early stimulation of this ability makes the acquisition of still other languages much easier for him. These are manifestations of mental processes that are uniquely human. Their physiological properties are almost completely unknown. Where and how the mind acquired these properties is open to even greater speculation.

So it is that the generative grammarian begins his investigation into the nature of English syntax believing that his key facts are to be found in the intuition of the native speaker of English. He knows that the origins of these intuitive processes are—and are likely to remain—unknown. The problem of origins besets every science, but it does not stop scientific investigation.

Generative grammar theory does not attempt to duplicate the workings of the human mind. Obviously it cannot, since these workings are an unknown quantity. But the competence is there, whether its physiological properties can be identified or not. Generative grammar theory does seek to present, according to its originator, Noam Chomsky, "a theory based on certain assumptions about the kinds of process that exist in language and the manner in which they interrelate."

The basic assumptions upon which the theory is based are these:

1.   All languages have a system of syntactic structure.

2.   Native speakers intuitively know the grammar of their language.

3.   In English, the basis of the system is something called the *sentence.*

All of the generative-grammar theory of the English language can be considered an attempt to define that single word.

What constitutes an English sentence? Shall we list endless patterns or shall we search for methods that will allow us to reuse certain patterns in different ways, show relationships between grammatical forms and make combinations in orderly ways?

In the field of mathematics a child does not need to memorize the multiples of numbers past 9×9. He does not need to have stored in his memory the fact that $126 \times 157 = 19,782$. After he learns the multiplication table up to 9×9, he is told to memorize a few very simple rules for reusing the basics he knows. He is shown how to carry numbers, how to shift multiplications answers for the digits in the first two places and then how to add the answers for each digit so that he gets something like this:

$$\begin{array}{r} 126 \\ \times 157 \\ \hline 882 \\ 630 \\ 126 \\ \hline 19,782 \end{array}$$

He can reuse his multiplication table in an infinite number of problems after he is given the rules for reusing them. These are called *recursive* rules. Modern mathematical instruction includes demonstrating for the student how such recursive systems are established so that he not only knows how to make mathematical computations but the rationale behind what he is doing.

The generative grammarian sets about his task of defining the English sentence in a similar way. First there are the *phrase structure rules* which describe the parts and relationships in simple, declarative sentences. These sentences are referred to as *the kernel*—the sentences that form the core of the language. Next, there are the *transformational rules* for changing these sentences into other forms, such as the passive, negative, yes-no questions, and so on.

Some of the phrase structure and transformational rules allow for the fact that simple sentences may be combined to form complex and compound types of sentences. When two sentences are combined, one is said to be *embedded* in the other. The rules for these processes are stated in such a way that they can be used and reused, embedding sentences into other sentences, layer after layer. Such rules allow repeated use of the phrase structure rules in infinite combination. They are, like the rules that allow the mathematician to use and reuse the multiplication table in multiplying numbers of two digits or more, said to be *recursive*.

Two sets of rules are basic: the phrase structure rules of the kernel sentences, and the transformational rules that may be applied to basic sentences to produce all the rest of the grammatical sentences in the language. Each of these rules is presented as a formula. It is not claimed that these formulas duplicate mental process, but only that they describe the results of mental process and show grammatical relationships in a concise way. It is also expected that, if the rules are properly stated, they will not allow the production of any ungrammatical sentences.

THE COMPONENTS OF A GENERATIVE GRAMMAR

Generative grammar deals with a series of grammatical relationships. These relationships are expressed in symbolic form. The symbols and combinations of symbols also define categories. In its original form, generative grammar consisted of three *components*. Each of these components, or parts, consisted of a set of rules: First, the phrase structure rules set up the grammatical categories and relationships of various categories in simple declarative sentences; second, the transformational rules set up formulas for converting the simple declarative sentences into other grammatical structures, such as phrases, clauses and other types of sentences; third, the morphophonemic rules recognized as necessary to show spoken and written forms of English sentences.

The use of symbols allows for presentation of categories and relationships in the clearest and simplest way possible. The phrase structure rules of a generative grammar begin with the notation $S \rightarrow NP$ VP. The information contained in these symbols is this: A kernel sentence in English consists of a noun phrase and a verb phrase. Either "phrase" may consist of a single word or several, but both the noun phrase and the verb phrase must be present. The noun phrase comes first. Therefore, a kernel sentence is made up of a noun phrase followed by a verb phrase; *sentence may be rewritten noun phrase plus verb phrase*. All of this is included in the symbolic notation $S \rightarrow NP$ VP. The little arrow is called a *rewrite arrow*.

The system of notation continues by expanding elements that appear to the right of the rewrite arrow. For example, the next two rewrite rules might take the form $NP \rightarrow D$ N (noun phrase may be rewritten determiner plus noun) and $VP \rightarrow A$ MV (verb phrase may be rewritten auxiliary plus main verb structure).

Often, those who are approaching the ideas of generative grammar for the first time show a reluctance to deal with these symbolic representations as tools in the classroom. These same people would have little patience with a recipe that began:

"Sift a large quantity of flour and measure out two cups full. Put one cup into the mixing bowl. Divide the remaining cup into four equal parts. Replace one part in the flour canister and put three parts into the mixing bowl . . ."

It is so much easier to deal with a recipe that makes use of a symbolic system and begins:

"1 3/4 c. sifted flour."

Even so, maintain the more reluctant of this group, there are so *many* symbols and relationships to be mastered in generative grammar. These are perfectly natural reactions to a quick confrontation with large portions of the theory without sufficient time to assimilate the detail.

In order to get some perspective on this problem, it is well to consider another complex system of symbols with which most of us are already familiar—the simple arithmetic taught at the elementary school level. The system includes the following points:

A. Numbers or quantities may be assigned to the symbols 0, 1, 2, 3, 4, 5, 6, 7, 8, 9.

B. There are ways of combining these symbols to represent larger quantities.
   The "tens place," the "hundreds place," and so forth. (A matter of relationships.)
   Commas are used to set off large numbers as in 1,000,000.
   0's are used as "place holders" as in 203, 1,040, and so forth.

C. Simple addition. The + symbol. The = symbol.
   Terms: *add, addition, plus, sum,* and *total.* (Utter confusion, two terms for the same thing!)

D. Addition of larger numbers.
   Beginning with the right-hand column. (Rules of order.)
   Carrying numbers.

E. Simple subtraction. The — symbol.
   Terms: *subtract, subtraction, minus, difference.*

F. Subtraction of larger numbers.

Beginning with the right-hand column.

Borrowing numbers.

Checking answers by addition. (More complex relationships.)

G. Simple multiplication. The $\times$ symbol.

Terms: *multiply, multiplication, multiplier, times.*

The multiplication table. (Involving such relationships as those shown by $3 \times 5 = 15$; $5 \times 3 = 15$.)

H. Multiplication of larger numbers.

Beginning with the right-hand digit of multiplier.

Carrying numbers again; reuse of addition. (More relationships and rules of order.)

I. Simple division. The $\div$ symbol.

Terms: *divide, divisor, dividend, quotient, remainder.*

Use of multiplication table in reverse, estimating . . . (More relationships.)

J. Division of larger numbers.

Beginning at the left-hand side of number to be divided.

Reuse of multiplication, subtraction, carrying and borrowing numbers. (Complex relationships.)

Checking answers by multiplication. (Relationships.)

K. Fractions. Symbolic placing of one number over another, as with ½ and ¼, to show relationships.

Terms: *numerator, denominator, half, fourth, quarter,* etc.

Reuse of addition, subtraction, multiplication and division, with new processes involved in each.

L. Decimals. The . symbol.

Relationships of numbers to the right and numbers to the left of the decimal point.

Relationships of these representations to fractions.

Reuse of addition, subtraction, multiplication, division.

M. Percentage. The % symbol.

New terms: *percentage, percent.*

Relationships of these representations to decimals and fractions. (While similar in many ways, fractions, decimals, and percentage each have areas of greater usefulness— choice between them rests on context or usage.)

N. Beyond this point are other elaborations such as algebra, which makes use of still other symbols and processes, but also makes use of basic arithmetic processes and relationships;

and geometry, with its angles, 360° circles, radius, diameter, circumference, arcs, and so on.

Exposed to the whole system without previous training, and given the task of teaching it, one might very well be expected to maintain stoutly that there are too many symbols and terms, too many complex relationships—and certainly no child could ever be expected to get beyond subtraction!

But all this is not a valid comparison, maintain our most reluctant teachers of English. The arithmetic teacher is not faced with problems of lexical meaning. She deals only in quantities. For many years, arithmetic teachers agreed and taught their subject matter by means of rote and drill. More recently, many have found that investigation of deeper considerations of meaning—such as those included in the teaching of set theory and numeration systems—help their students to a firmer grasp of the principles of mathematics.

All this does not mean that language can be taught as mathematics is taught. Language cannot be mechanized any more than the human brain can be mechanized. Grammatical categories may be symbolized, but we do not speak categories. We speak words, which are the members of categories. Teachers may deal in categories, but they must also deal with such things as lexical meaning, spoken forms, and the written representation of those spoken forms. The teacher or the linguistic scholar cannot simply organize a system that allows for no deviation from rigid rules. Such a system would require, for example, the discarding of irregular plurals and irregular verb forms. These and other problems must be recognized and dealt with as methodically as possible.

Recognition of the special problems of teaching language does not mean that we cannot use symbol systems, but it does set some limitations on how we use them and what results we can expect.

Generative grammar, as we have said, deals with categories and relationships of these categories. Consideration of other language problems must fall into other components of a complete description of English. One of these components might deal with category members. In some cases, such as the modals, these categories have comparatively few members; in others, such as the noun, they have an enormous, ever-increasing number of members. Lists of these members may be seen as the final step in the phrase structure rules or, since they deal with category members rather than categories, they may be set apart. When they are set apart, they are referred to as the *lexicon,* and the lexicon becomes another component or subcomponent of the grammar. Further elaboration of the description of the grammar to include phonemic representation of spoken forms or graphemic representations of written forms might be included as still other components of a complete description of the grammar of English.

Some clarification of the components may be gained by consideration of some simple examples of what each component is designed to accomplish.

In the case of the first component, the phrase structure rules, one highly simplified set of symbols describing kernel sentences might include the following:

			Symbols:	
PS Rule 1	$S \rightarrow NP \quad VP$		S	sentence
PS Rule 2	$NP \rightarrow D \quad N$		NP	noun phrase
PS Rule 3	$VP \rightarrow \begin{Bmatrix} be & Pred \\ MV \end{Bmatrix}$		VP	verb phrase
			D	determiner
PS Rule 4	$MV \rightarrow \begin{Bmatrix} V_T & NP \\ V_I \\ V_L & C \end{Bmatrix}$		N	noun
			be	the verb *be*
			MV	main verb
			V_T	transitive verb
			V_I	intransitive verb
			V_L	linking verb
			C	complement

Braces enclose rewrite choices. Where choices appear in braces, one and only one line of symbols must be chosen from the alternatives that appear in the braces.

Choosing the second rewrite possibility of VP and the first rewrite possibility of MV, we can combine the rules given for a final or *terminal string* of symbols for one possible kernel sentence in English:

$$D \quad N \quad V_T \quad D \quad N$$

Note that the NP rewrite, Rule 2, has been used twice.

These rules, as we have said, not only serve to show syntactic relationships but also serve to define categories. The definitions of types of main verb structures at this stage of the description are: transitive verb is followed by a noun phrase; intransitive verb is followed by nothing; and linking verb is followed by a complement. Further distinctions are made as the rules are expanded. These definitions are virtually the same as those of traditional grammar: A transitive verb takes a direct object; an intransitive verb does not take an object; and a linking, or copulative verb takes a complement. The difference at this point is only in the simplification and ease of comparison afforded by setting the symbols side by side.

A second component of a generative grammar of English involves the symbolizing of other types of structures, and other types of sentences, such as the passive. Rather than begin all over again with a rewrite of *passive sentences,* it is simpler to work out rules that transform the items in the terminal strings of kernel sentences. This not only allows us to bypass a lot of preliminaries but also to gain another insight into the grammatical relationships of our categories.

Given the terminal string derived above, and noting the order of the D and N symbols, we would have:

$$D_1 \quad N_1 \quad V_T \quad D_2 \quad N_2$$

A simple passive transform might order changes that would result in the following order for a string of symbols that would generate a passive sentence from the terminal string above:

$$D_2 \quad N_2 \quad \textit{be} \quad V_T \quad \textit{by} \quad D_1 \quad N_1$$

Using still another component of the grammar, the lexicon, we might make a variety of lexical substitutions for the symbols. The lexicon lists members of categories symbolized. Any member of each category may be chosen so that the PS terminal string above could generate an enormous number of possible lexical strings.

The lexicon might provide the following word-members for the categories that appear in the terminal string above:

D $\to$ *a, an, the, . . .*
N $\to$ *boy, girl, dog, cat, stones, . . .*
$V_T \to$ *eat, throw, chase, . . .*

Making sample substitutions, we might generate the following sentences from the terminal string D N V_T D N:

1. The boy threw the stones.
2. The dog chased a cat.

The transformational rule orders that, if these sentences are to be changed into passive sentences, certain elements—the determiners and nouns—must be shifted, and that a form of the word *be* and the word *by* must be added in certain positions. Similar lexical substitutions for the string of category symbols we arrived at by applying the transformational rule would result in:

T-1.   The stones were thrown by the boy.
T-2.   A cat was chased by the dog.

A component of the grammar devoted to written forms in English would dictate the spellings used here as well as the fact that the first letter in each sentence is a capital and that a period appears at the end of each sentence.

Still another component of the grammar would be needed for specifying spoken forms of the category members, or words, chosen above. Making use of the phonemic alphabet covered earlier for this purpose, we might arrive at the following transcriptions of the passive sentences above:

T-1.   /ðə stownz wər θrown bay ðə boy/

T-2.   /ə kæt wəz čeyst bay ðə dɔgz/

Components of a generative grammar, then, include (1) phrase structure rules; (2) transformational rules; and (3) a lexicon. Greater detail is added by components made up of (4) morphophonemic rules, which specify pronunciation or speech forms of the items in the lexicon; and (5) morphographemic rules, which specify the written forms of the lexical items and sentences. Some who make use of generative grammar methods in describing English include rules of order as a separate component of the grammar; others include notations of order in the phrase structure rules.

The phrase structure rules and diagraming

As the phrase structure rules are developed and expanded, it will become apparent that this description of the syntactic structure of English has much in common with immediate constituent analysis. In IC analysis of a simple, declarative sentence, the first cut or division is between subject and predicate; the first PS rule is S → NP VP. In this and each succeeding PS rule, the symbol for only one category or structure appears to the left of the rewrite arrow. Those symbols to the right of the arrow may be seen to represent the constituents of the structure being rewritten or detailed. The procedure continues until the final or terminal string of constituent symbols is reached.

The process of deriving the terminal string can be charted step by step, rule by rule, as demonstrated by the simplified set of rules presented on page 130 and the diagraming of the sentence we derived ending in the terminal string D N V_T D N.

Our step by step procedure can be diagramed.

Use of PS Rule 1   S → NP VP:

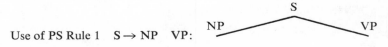

Use of PS Rule 2   NP → D   N:

Choice from
PS Rule 3   VP → MV:

Choice from
PS Rule 4   MV → V_T   NP:

Reuse of
PS Rule 2   NP → D   N:

Symbols are then brought
down to show the
Terminal String:

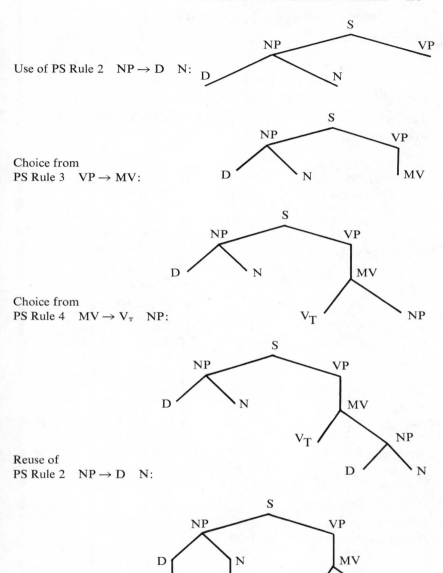

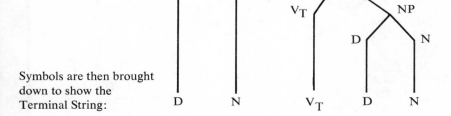

If we add, as PS Rule 5, that a predicate may be either an adjective or a noun phrase:

$$\text{SP Rule 5} \quad \text{Pred} \rightarrow \begin{Bmatrix} \text{Aj} \\ \text{NP} \end{Bmatrix}$$

then we might make the following steps to derive still another terminal string:

Use of PS Rule 1	S → NP VP
Use of PS Rule 2	NP → D N
Choice from PS Rule 3	VP → *be* Pred
Choice from PS Rule 5	Pred → NP
Reuse of PS Rule 2	NP → D N

This list of steps coincides to the diagram below.

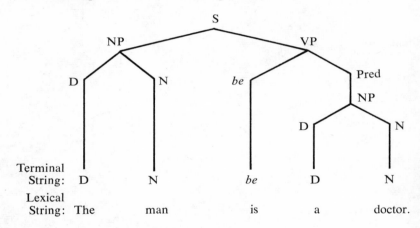

This kind of diagraming, often called branching-tree diagraming, leaves the sentence in its spoken or written order and, in addition, clearly labels categories and relationships.

11

THE
PHRASE STRUCTURE
RULES

The first component of a generative grammar of English is concerned with the phrase structure rules. These begin with the concept that the sentence is the basis of the syntactic system used by speakers of English.

The phrase structure rules describe the least complicated of English sentences. These are simple, declarative, affirmative, indicative sentences —which is a rather elaborate way of excluding questions, negative sentences, passive sentences, those with compound elements, and so on. Continued reference to our basic sentences as "simple, declarative, affirmative, indicative" would be rather cumbersome. We shall call them —as the generative grammarian does—*kernel* sentences.

The designation *kernel* applied to these sentences also identifies them as those sentences which make up the core of the language. All other sentences in the language are assumed to be transformations of kernel sentences.

The phrase structure rules break the category S—for kernel sentence—into its principal constituents and note the sequence, or relationship, of these constituents to each other. The basic constituents of a kernel sentence are identified as structures called an NP—for noun phrase—and a VP—for verb phrase. Their relationship is described by their position in the formula. The NP which precedes a VP in the rules functions as subject of the sentence; the VP then functions as predicate of the sentence. Later we will find that some types of verbs are *followed* by an NP. Such a difference in position indicates a difference in function.

What this means is simply that in a sentence such as

The hat is pretty.

The hat is a noun phrase that functions as subject of the sentence, while in a sentence such as

Sally bought the hat.

the hat is a noun phrase that functions as object of the verb. In each case, the function of the NP is determined by its position in relation to the other parts of the sentence. *The phrase structure rules, then, identify structures by assigning a symbol to each, and identify functions by placing the symbols in a sequence that describes their relationship to each other.*

We shall begin with a few basic PS rules. These will be slightly more detailed than those that we have considered before, but they are still greatly simplified for purposes of clarity. It is important to note that there is no universally accepted numbering system for phrase structure rules. The numbers given to the rules here are only for purposes of discussing the rules in the text that follows.

Phrase Structure Rules	Symbols for Structures:	
PS Rule 1 S → NP VP	S	kernel sentence
	NP	noun phrase
PS Rule 2 NP → $\left\{\begin{matrix} D & N \\ Pron \end{matrix}\right\}$	VP	verb phrase
	D	determiner
PS Rule 3 VP → A MV	N	noun
PS Rule 4 A → t	Pron	pronoun
	A	auxiliary
PS Rule 5 t → $\left\{\begin{matrix} pres \\ past \end{matrix}\right\}$	t	tense
(→ means "consists of"	pres	common present tense
{ } means choose one	past	common past tense
line of symbols)	MV	main verb structure

These very fundamental phrase structure rules make several important points about the structure of kernel sentences in English. PS Rule 1, S → NP VP, says that a kernel sentence in English is made up of a noun phrase and a verb phrase and that the noun phrase comes first.

PS Rule 2, NP → $\left\{\begin{matrix} D & N \\ Pron \end{matrix}\right\}$, says that every noun phrase con-

tains a determiner and a noun—in that order—*or* a pronoun.

PS Rule 3, VP → A MV, says that every verb phrase contains an auxiliary plus a main verb structure; and PS Rule 4, A → t, says that a part of the auxiliary is the tense factor or morpheme in English verbs. Greater detail will be added to the auxiliary later.

PS Rule 5, $t \rightarrow \begin{Bmatrix} \text{pres} \\ \text{past} \end{Bmatrix}$, completes the specification that the auxiliary that appears in every kernel sentence in English includes a factor of tense. Every verb phrase includes a present or a past tense morpheme. In some cases the auxiliary may, in some cases it may not include other forms, but, for the moment, we shall consider only the absolutely required factor of verb tense.

Charting rules 1–5 and choosing a determiner plus a noun from PS Rule 2, and the present tense from PS Rule 5, results in the branching-tree diagram and terminal string shown below.

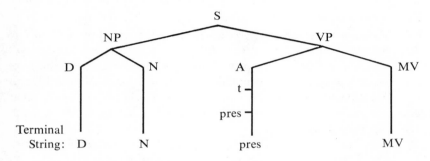

If we continue our breakdown of categories, it would seem only natural to begin with further detail in the noun phrase because our very first PS rule tells us that it always appears first in kernel sentences. Most generative grammarians do begin with detail in the noun phrase. Such a plan will not be followed here for two reasons. First, the PS rules are designed to describe the kernel sentences of English. The makeup of these sentences is clearer if we consider various types of sentences and those factors which define the different kernel sentence types are to be found in the verb phrase. Second, several very good arguments in favor of generative grammar as a useful and effective description of English syntax are most easily demonstrated to a beginner by means of investigation of the verb phrase rules.

12

THE VERB PHRASE

Any teacher who has had the experience of plodding dutifully through a stack of student compositions with red pencil at the ready is well aware that deviation from standard verb usage is one of the most easily recognized of all student problems. Many students make the same mistakes again and again. Can generative grammar bring some new light to this area of confusion? If so, is it teachable in simplified form? What does generative grammar have to offer in explanation of the English verb that may be useful?

It is not necessary to belabor the point that traditional grammar sought to describe the English verb by means of a Latin grammar pattern. Nevertheless, the fact is that Latin verbs and English verbs operate in very different ways. Unlike the traditionalist, the generative grammarian is willing to forego the supposed superiority of the logic of Latin grammar. He is concerned with describing the logic of the English language as it exists—as it is used by speakers of English. How does the generative grammarian deal with English verbs?

There are several types of kernel sentences in English. All are a part of the kernel; all are called kernel sentences. The differences between these types of kernel sentences can be shown without changing the noun phrase. For example, the sentences below are all kernel sentences in English:

A. The boy is tall.
B. The boy is my brother.
C. The boy is here.
D. The boy smiled.
E. The boy ate the cookies.
F. The boy gave the girl a cookie.

G. The boy became friendly.

H. The boy became the leader.

I. The boy has a car.

Each is a different type of kernel sentence.

Obviously the noun phrase, too, can take other forms, but these different forms may be listed at great length without changing the sentence type. For example:

J. The boy is tall.

K. They are tall.

L. These two gentlemen are tall.

M. Some of the girls are tall.

N. The first two of the last six students are tall.

Each represents differences in detail of a single sentence type. We will consider the variations possible in the noun phrase at some length later. For the moment, it will be easier to gain a broad view of the types of sentences that make up the kernel if we consider the nine most common sentence types which are exemplified by sentences A–I above.

The PS rules will be extended to account for these sentences and others like them. The rules will be diagramed and terminal strings shown for each sentence type. It is obvious that substitution of other lexical items for the category symbols of the terminal strings would result in an enormous variety of sentences in English.

The PS rules we will use for a further breakdown of the verb phrase will continue the numbering begun on page 136. The rules are these:

Phrase Structure Rules   *Sentence Patterns*

$$\text{PS Rule 6 } MV \rightarrow \begin{Bmatrix} be \quad \text{Pred} \\ V \end{Bmatrix}$$

—Choice necessary for A, B, C
—Choice necessary for D–I

$$\text{PS Rule 7 } \text{Pred} \rightarrow \begin{Bmatrix} \text{Aj} \\ \text{NP} \\ \text{Av-p} \end{Bmatrix}$$

—Pattern A
—Pattern B
—Pattern C

$$\text{PS Rule 8 } V \rightarrow \begin{Bmatrix} \begin{matrix} V_I \\ V_T \quad NP \quad (NP) \\ V_L \begin{Bmatrix} Aj \\ NP \end{Bmatrix} \end{matrix} (Av\text{-}m) \\ V_H \quad NP \end{Bmatrix}$$

—Pattern D
—Patterns E, F
—Pattern G
—Pattern H
—Pattern I

Symbols Used

MV	main verb structure	V	verb structure
be	form of the verb *be*	V_I	intransitive verb
Pred	predicate	V_T	transitive verb
Aj	adjective	V_L	linking verb
NP	noun phrase	V_H	verb of the *have* type
Av-p	adverb of place	Av-m	adverb of manner
( )	Parentheses mark an item that may or may not be chosen.		

These rules appear terribly complex at first glance, but translation of the symbols, rule by rule, serves to make them less formidable.

In order to reiterate the crucial importance of the concept that verb tense is a part of every verb phrase in every kernel sentence in English, and the means by which generative grammarians establish this concept in their notations, we must return to PS Rules 3, 4, and 5 which were given on page 136.

PS Rule 3 notes that every verb phrase of every kernel sentence in English has two principal constituents. These are the auxiliary and the main verb structure.

PS Rule 3	VP	$\rightarrow$	A	MV
	every verb phrase of every kernel sentence in English	may be rewritten	auxiliary	main verb structure

The complete description of the syntax of English requires that we note clearly and specifically—at the earliest stage possible—that verb tense is a basic requirement in any English sentence. As noted earlier, the auxiliary may or may not contain other forms as well, but they are not necessary for establishing the distinctions between types of kernel sentences. For the moment we have enough categories to consider; we will leave other auxiliary forms until later.

PS Rule 4 notes that the auxiliary includes the factor of verb tense.

PS Rule 4	A	$\rightarrow$	t
	auxiliary	may be rewritten	tense morpheme

PS Rule 5 notes that there are two tense forms in English and that these are present and past tense forms. One or the other is a part of every auxiliary in every kernel sentence.

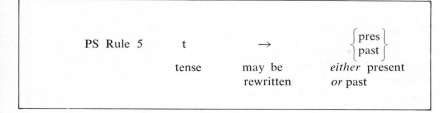

PS Rule 6 notes that a main verb structure in a kernel sentence in English may consist of a structure headed by a form of the verb *be* followed by a predicate, or it may consist of a structure headed by some other verb.

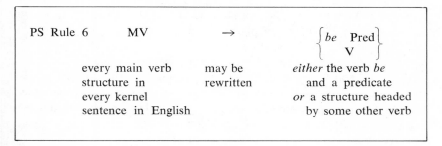

The major point made in this notation is that there is a fundamental difference between the verb *be* and all other verbs in English. This rule indicates that the difference is so great that *be* cannot be listed as a subcategory further down the line, but must be considered a category unto itself from this point of classification onward. As we progress to further description of the kernel sentences and, still later, when we consider how various kernel sentences may be transformed into other structures, the differences in the behavior of the category *be* will become more clearly defined.

PS Rule 7 lists the forms that may be taken by the predicate necessary to complete a kernel sentence in which *be* heads the main verb structure.

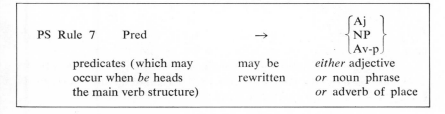

PS Rule 8 sorts all the other verbs of English into four categories. These categories are, from top to bottom, V_I for intransitive verbs; V_T for transitive verbs; V_L for linking verbs; and V_H for verbs of the *have* type. In a highly detailed description of English syntax, these categories might be further subdivided at some length with peculiarities of environment noted to define, for example, different types of transitive verbs. For purposes of describing rather broad categories that include the most common types of sentences in the kernel, the four categories above will serve.

All of the first three types listed—the intransitive, transitive and linking verbs—may or may not be followed by an adverb of manner. Adverbs of manner include such forms as *quickly, reluctantly,* and *quietly*. These adverbs of manner are optional—they may or may not be chosen—to complete a verb structure headed by intransitive, transitive and linking verbs. The optional nature of this category is shown in the notation by means of placing it in parentheses.

In sentences A–I, listed for demonstrating the most common types of kernel sentences, no adverbs of manner were chosen for sentences D, E, F, G, and H, but these sentences demonstrate the use of intransitive, transitive, and linking verbs, and adverbs of manner may be added to them without changing the sentence types. The sentences with adverbs would simply be alternate choices to the sentences without them. For example:

The boy ate the cookies.
The boy ate the cookies quietly.

Both sentences are of the type we have designated Pattern E.

One of the four categories of verbs, the category which we have called verbs of the *have* type and to which we have assigned the symbol V_H, is defined by the fact that the sentence type in which it appears will *not* admit the addition of an adverb of manner. Addition of adverbs of manner to the example sentence given for Pattern I results in such ungrammatical sequences as

*The boy has a car quickly.
*The boy has a car reluctantly.

Have is the most frequently used member of the category, but the category does have other members, such as *weigh* and *cost*.

Having set off, and thus defined, one of our four categories, we may now turn to the task of defining the remaining three categories.

The rule notes that intransitive verbs, V_I, may stand alone as the entire verb structure of the kernel sentences in which they appear; transitive verbs, V_T, must be followed by a noun phrase and may or may not be followed by two noun phrases; and linking verbs, V_L, may be followed by either an adjective or a noun phrase. Each of these categories might be further subdivided to sort its members into still more definitive subcategories. For example, some transitive verbs will not take both a direct and an indirect object; some form sentences that may be transformed into passive sentences while others do not, and some demand certain types of objects. We will not attempt such sub-classification but simply note that it would be a part of a full description of English syntax.

Verbs, like all other categories, are classified or put into categories by the environments in which they may appear. The categories in our simplified PS Rule 8 are defined in this way.

PS Rule 8				
V	$\rightarrow$	$\left\{\begin{array}{l} V_I \\ V_T \quad NP \ (NP) \\ V_L \ \left\{\begin{array}{l} Aj \\ NP \end{array}\right\} \\ V_H \end{array}\right.$	(Av-m)	
a verb headed structure	may be rewritten	*either* intransitive verb *or* transitive verb and one or two noun phrases *or* a linking verb and *either* an adjective *or* a noun phrase *or* a verb of the *have* type and a noun phrase	which may or may not be followed by an adverb of manner which may *not* be followed by an adverb of manner	

Example sentences A–I may be used to represent the sentence patterns resulting from the three possible uses of *be* plus a predicate; the use of an intransitive verb; the two possible uses of transitive verbs; the two possible uses of linking verbs; and the use of a verb of the *have* type. Both terminal strings and lexical strings are shown.

A.   D N pres *be* Aj   (*be*   plus   predicate
       [The boy is   tall.]   where predicate is
                                    an adjective)

B.   D N   pres *be* D   N   (*be* plus predicate
         [The boy   is   my   brother.]   where predicate is
                                                  a noun phrase)

C.   D N   pres *be* Av-p   (*be* plus predicate
         [The boy   is   here.]   where predicate is
                                                  an adverb of place)

D.   D N   past V$_I$ (intransitive verb)
         [The boy   smiled.]

E.   D N   past V$_T$ D   N   (transitive verb plus a
         [The boy   ate   the   cookies.]   noun phrase)

F.   D N   past V$_T$ D N D   N   (transitive verb plus
         [The boy   gave the girl a cookie.]   two noun phrases)

G.   D N   past V$_L$ Aj   (linking verb plus an
         [The boy   became friendly.]   adjective)

H.   D N   past V$_L$ D   N   (linking verb plus a
         [The boy   became the leader.]   noun phrase)

I.   D N   pres V$_H$ D   N   (*have* type verb plus
         [The boy   has   a   car.]   a noun phrase)

The strings of category symbols called terminal strings, result from combination of the PS rules. Lexical substitutions for the categories have been made here arbitrarily. Other substitutions are possible. Given the several hundred thousand nouns, verbs, and adjectives in the English language, it is apparent that these rules will generate an enormous number of lexical strings. With the rules for embedding sentences into other sentences that we will take up in the chapters that follow, the number of sentences possible will be literally infinite.

Diagraming the step-by-step application of the PS rules for sentences A, B, D, and E will result in the patterns shown below. Trace the application of successive PS rules that result in patterns C, F, G, H, and I in the same way using the diagrams below as guidelines.

Pattern A

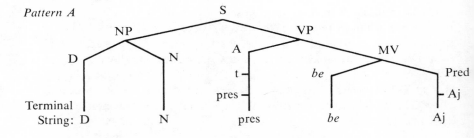

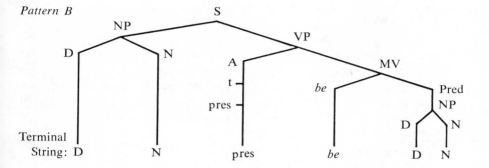

Pattern B

Terminal String: D N pres *be* D N

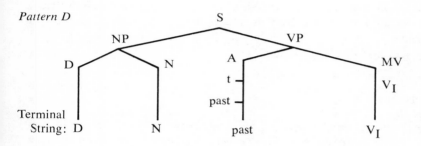

Pattern D

Terminal String: D N past V$_I$

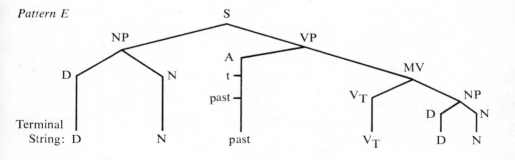

Pattern E

Terminal String: D N past V$_T$ D N

THE COMPLETE AUXILIARY RULE

The generative grammarian defines the auxiliary as consisting of *tense*—either a past or present morpheme—and other forms which may or may not be present before the main verb structure in kernel sentences. The notation describing the complete auxiliary in English kernel sentences is this:

$$A \rightarrow t \quad (M) \quad (have + \text{-en}) \quad (be + \text{-ing})$$

The category symbols added here are the M, which stands for modal; *have,* for the auxiliary word *have;* -en, for the past participle morpheme that always appears when a form of the auxiliary *have* appears in a kernel sentence in English; be, for the auxiliary word *be;* and -ing, for the present participle morpheme that always appears when a form of the auxiliary word *be* appears in a kernel sentence in English. The most common English modals are *can, may, must, shall,* and *will.*

The auxiliary rewrite, or PS rule, notes that the auxiliary must include a tense morpheme; that this may or may not be followed by a modal; that the optional modal may or may not be followed by a combination of the auxiliary *have* and an -en, or past participle morpheme; and that this combination may or may not be followed by a combination of the auxiliary *be* and an -ing, or present participle, morpheme.

Considered item by item:

PS Rule 4					
A	$\rightarrow$	t	(M)	(*have* + *-en*)	(*be* + *-ing*)
auxiliary	may be rewritten	tense morpheme	a modal may or may not be chosen	*have* and an -en morpheme may or may not be chosen	*be* and an -ing morpheme may or may not be chosen

Some of the uses of this rule are demonstrated below. A simple NP—with lexical substitution *the boys* has been used, together with the modal *may,* and the simplest possible main verb structure, a transitive verb with the lexical substitution *eat,* which allows deletion of a direct object. When dashes (—) appear, they indicate that an optional item has not been chosen.

Auxiliary combinations possible are:

NP		(*M*)	(*have* + *-en*)	(*be* + *-ing*)	
NP The boys	pres	—	—	—	V_T eat.
NP The boys	past	—	—	—	V_T ate.
NP The boys	pres → M may		—	—	V_T eat.
NP The boys	past → M might		—	—	V_T eat.

NP	pres	—	have + -en	—	V_T
The boys			have		eaten.

NP	past	—	have + -en	—	V_T
The boys			had		eaten.

NP	pres	M	have + -en	—	V_T
The boys		may	have		eaten.

NP	past	M	have + -en	—	V_T
The boys		might	have		eaten.

NP	pres	—	—	be + -ing	V_T
The boys				are	eating.

NP	past	—	—	be + -ing	V_T
The boys				were	eating.

NP	pres	M	—	be + -ing	V_T
The boys		may		be	eating.

NP	past	M	—	be + -ing	V_T
The boys		might		be	eating.

NP	pres	—	have + -en	be + -ing	V_T
The boys			have	been	eating.

NP	past	—	have + -en	be + -ing	V_T
The boys			had	been	eating.

NP	pres	M	have + -en	be + -ing	V_T
The boys		may	have	been	eating.

NP	past	M	have + -en	be + -ing	V_T
The boys		might	have	been	eating.

We have used a single modal, *may,* and a single transitive verb, *eat.* All of this would apply, in the same way, to any choice of modals and any choice of verb in any kernel sentence in English. It applies whether the NP is first, second or third person, singular or plural.

Third person singular NP's dictate a particular present tense morpheme that is applied to the auxiliary and verb forms, and the auxiliary *be,* like the verb *be,* has a unique set of forms that depend upon the choice of NP. Since these are tied to the NP, their use is included in a rule dealing with the NP rather than the auxiliary. All other factors are a part of the auxiliary system and all are contained in the notation

$$A \rightarrow t \quad (M) \quad (have + -en) \quad (be + ing)$$

The teacher who is firmly grounded in traditional definitions of the past, present, future, past perfect, present perfect, future perfect, emphatic, and progressive tenses—or some variation on this list—will find that all notional definitions are missing here and will, perhaps, consider this only skimming the surface of the grammar of English. What is to be gained by teaching students how the standard dialect manipulates forms if the consideration of meaning is ignored? The answer is that a study of the system of grammar becomes more than the simple prescribing of rules when approached in this way. It becomes, instead, a tool for exploring the language.

In Latin, each of the ways in which the meaning of a verb may be qualified is denoted by a suffix. Conjugations are, therefore, useful lists of suffixes together with the type of qualification each brings to a verb stem.

In English, the verb system works in quite another way. Verbs are qualified by morphemic changes to the verb stem, or by the use of auxiliary forms or both. When both occur, as in the case of the auxiliary *have* and the *-en* morpheme, they may be said to be, in fact, a single form made up of discontinuous elements. The modals, *can, may, shall, will, must, need, ought to,* and so on, are different from the auxiliary forms *have* and *be* in that they bring no other elements with them into the kernel strings. They differ also in the fact that their meaning relates as much to the subject of the sentence as it does to the verb stem. Modals actually have a foot in each camp since the meanings, that is, compulsion, desire, intent, and so on, are attributable to the subject but, at the same time, the most common modals also accept past and present morphemes as do other auxiliary forms.

	+ *present*	+ *past*	+ *-en*	+ *-ing*
can	can	could		
may	may	might		
shall	shall	should		
will	will	would		
be	am	was	been	being
	are	were		
	is			
have	have	had	had	having
	has			
eat	eat	ate	eaten	eating
	eats			
love	love	loved	loved	loving
	loves			
sing	sing	sang	sung	singing
	sings			
walk	walk	walked	walked	walking
	walks			

(NOTE: *be* is unusual in that it has a special second person singular present tense form and a plural past tense form. Like other verbs, it has a special third person singular present tense form. The use of these forms is, of course, dictated by the person and number of the subject. All other forms are dictated by the choices made in the auxiliary.)

If students can be shown the symmetry of the standard usage of the auxiliary forms in a simple, easily grasped way, then they are in control of that much. The next step is one that is concerned with semantics, but there is *something* upon which to build. Using the chart of combinations on pages 146–147, it is not difficult for the teacher to create discovery procedures. For example, what nuances of meaning occur when a modal is chosen that do not occur when a modal is not chosen? What differences are there between combinations using the past and present tense? (The teacher may find, along with the students, that forms of English verbs might better be classed as present and non-present, and thereby gain some insight into how English manages to get along quite nicely without a true future tense!) It is easier to base clear concepts of meaning on a sure knowledge of structure than it is to base definitions of structure on the shifting sands of meaning.

Compare the system specified by the PS rule for the English auxiliary with the conjugation of the English verb *love* on pages 150–151. The conjugation of the Latin verb *amāre* (to love) is included so that the complex system of inflections added to the Latin stem may be compared with the English system.

The PS rule for the auxiliary also provides an example of how a teacher can demonstrate, for those students who may speak a nonstandard dialect, the differences between the student's systematic usage and the standard system. Most nonstandard use of the auxiliary system omits items from the standard as expressed in the PS rule used here. The most commonly omitted item is the auxiliary form *have,* as in the nonstandard sentences:

> They been eating.
> I been trying.
> I been wishing.

Students who make this omission can be shown where their system differs from the standard if they are shown the auxiliary rewrite rule as a "short cut" to standard use of the auxiliary. They may be shown where they *systematically* differ, and thus given a guide to future use rather than random "corrections."

When speech forms are considered, the nonstandard omission is seen in a slightly different light. Informally, most speakers of English say "They've been eating," "We've been trying," and so on, reducing the *have* to a single phoneme, /v/. For more formal usage, this is easily shifted back into the form *have*. The nonstandard dialect has dropped the /v/ in informal speech and has thus cut the bridge back to the formal usage.

COMPARISON OF CONJUGATIONS

	LATIN *amāre*	ENGLISH *love*	
	Indicative		
Pres	amō	I love, am loving, do love	we love, are loving, do love
	amās	you love, are loving, do love	you love, are loving, do love
	amat	he loves, is loving, does love	they love, are loving, do love
Impf	amābam	I was loving	we were loving
	amābās	you were loving	you were loving
	amābat	he was loving	they were loving
Fut	amābō	I shall love, shall be loving	we shall love, shall be loving
	amābis	you will love, will be loving	you will love, will be loving
	amābit	he will love, will be loving	they will love, will be loving
Perf	amāvī	I loved, have loved	we loved, have loved
	amāvistī	you loved, have loved	you loved, have loved
	amāvit	he loved, has loved	they loved, have loved
Plup	amāveram	I had loved	we had loved
	amāverās	you had loved	you had loved
	amāverat	he had loved	they had loved
Fut Perf	amāverō	I shall have loved	we shall have loved
	amāveris	you will have loved	you will have loved
	amāverit	he will have loved	they will have loved
	amāverimus		
	amāveritis		
	amāverint		

Subjunctive

Pres	amem	amēmus	I may love	we may love
	amēs	amētis	you may love	you may love
	amet	ament	he may love	they may love
Impf	amārem	amārēmus	I might love	we might love
	amārēs	amārētis	you might love	you might love
	amāret	amārent	he might love	they might love
Perf	amāverim	amāverimus	I may have loved	we may have loved
	amāveris	amāveritis	you may have loved	you may have loved
	amāverit	amāverint	he may have loved	they may have loved
Plup	amāvissem	amāvissēmus	I might have loved	we might have loved
	amāvissēs	amāvissētis	you might have loved	you might have loved
	amāvisset	amāvissent	he might have loved	they might have loved

The chart above translates Latin verb forms into English forms. Note the use of English modals *shall*, *will*, and *may*. How are they used in English? What of other English modals such as *can* and *must*? Inflections added to the English verb include the *-d* ending for both past tense and past participle (or *-en*) form, the *-ing* for the present participle form, and a single instance of *-s* for the present third person singular. Count the Latin inflections.

An attentive teacher, equipped with the auxiliary rewrite rule, can locate other dialect differences and point them out to the student.

The Affix Transformation

The curved arrows used in the chart on pages 146–147 indicate a need to shift elements of the auxiliary around if a grammatical sentence is to be derived. The string of symbols

$$t \quad M \quad \text{have} + \text{-en} \quad \text{be} + \text{-ing} \quad V_T$$

will not result in a grammatical string unless (1) tense is added to the verb phrase item that follows it; (2) the *-en* is added to the verb phrase item that follows it; and (3) *-ing* is added to the verb phrase item that follows it.

The tense morpheme, the *-en* morpheme, and the *-ing* morpheme are things that must be added, or affixed, to other items. They are, therefore, referred to as affixes and such affixes are symbolized by *Af*. The items in the verb phrase that will accept these affixes are the modals, the auxiliary forms *have* and *be,* and all types of verbs including the *be* category. All forms capable of accepting the affixes are called *v* forms. These may be identified below the string of category symbols:

t	M	have	-en	be	-ing	V_T
Af	v	v	Af	v	Af	v

Each instance of <u>Af   v</u> must be transposed and this is a form of transformation. In order to note this shifting of elements, another symbol is used for the notion "transform to." The symbol is a double-barred arrow, $\Rightarrow$.

The notation Af   v $\Rightarrow$ v   Af means that in each instance where an affix form is followed by a *v* form, their order must be reversed, or flopped over.

In the string of symbols used as an example, three applications of this Affix Transformation are required:

t	M	have	-en	be	-ing	V_T
<u>Af</u>	<u>v</u>	v	<u>Af</u>	<u>v</u>	<u>Af</u>	<u>v</u>

Applying the rule to each of the three instances, we have

M	t	have	be	-en	V_T	-ing
v	Af	v	v	Af	v	Af

THE VERB PHRASE 153

This leaves us with two new instances of an affix followed by a *v* form. But the affixes are now in their proper places. To prevent them from happily leapfrogging their way over every *v* form in the string, the rule must include a stop signal at the end of the first shift. The signal used is the word-final symbol #. The Affix Transformation rule then reads: Af v ⇒ v Af #.

Applying this transformational rule to the example string works like this:

$$
\begin{array}{cccccccc}
\text{t} & \text{M} & \text{have} & \text{-en} & \text{be} & \text{-ing} & V_T \\
\underline{\text{Af}} & \underline{\text{v}} & \text{v} & \underline{\text{Af}} & \underline{\text{v}} & \underline{\text{Af}} & \underline{\text{v}}
\end{array}
$$

Apply the rule Af v ⇒ v Af # for the transformed string:

$$
\begin{array}{ccccccc}
\text{M} & \text{t} & \text{have} & \text{be} & \text{-en} & V_T & \text{-ing} \\
\text{v} & \text{Af\#} & \text{v} & \text{v} & \text{Af\#} & \text{v} & \text{Af\#}
\end{array}
$$

Everything is now in proper order with no confusing <u>Af v</u> sequences remaining.

The Affix Transformation applies no matter what combination of elements is found in the terminal string. For example:

$$
\begin{array}{cccc}
\text{t} & \text{have} & \text{-en} & V_I \\
\underline{\text{Af}} & \underline{\text{v}} & \underline{\text{Af}} & \underline{\text{v}}
\end{array}
$$

Apply the rule

$$
\underline{\text{Af}\quad \text{v} \Rightarrow \text{v}\quad \text{Af\#}}
$$

for the transformed string

$$
\begin{array}{cccc}
\text{have} & \text{t} & V_I & \text{-en} \\
\text{v} & \text{Af\#} & \text{v} & \text{Af\#}
\end{array}
$$

For other examples, refer to the chart of other possible combinations of auxiliary and verb elements on pages 146–147 and work out the application of the affix transformation rule necessary to arrive at the final grammatical order.

Why is it necessary to put these elements into the phrase structure rules in one sequence and immediately establish a means of reordering them? If we are looking for a simpler description of English grammar, would it not be more economical to explore other means of writing them into the PS rules?

In order to understand the extremely sound basis for this analysis of the English auxiliary, we must explore the workings of auxiliary forms in some depth. In the auxiliary rewrite rule, the auxiliary form *have* is immediately followed by the *-en* or past participle morpheme. They are further bound together by the fact that the parentheses enclosing the two demands that using one forces use of the other. But the *-en* morpheme *never* follows the auxiliary *have* in a sentence spoken by a native speaker of English. The immediate relationship never appears on the surface, but the fact that a very real connection exists between the auxiliary form *have* and the past participle morpheme *-en* is easily demonstrated by a few kernel sentence examples taken from the chart on pages 146–147:

> The boys *have* eat*en*.
> The boys might *have* eat*en*.
> The boys *have* be*en* eating.
> The boys may *have* be*en* eating.

Whenever the auxiliary *have* appears in a kernel sentence it brings along an *-en* morpheme that must be affixed somewhere.

By anticipating a few transforms that we will discuss later, we can see that the close association between *have* and *-en* holds throughout the language. Consider the sentences

> *Have* the boys eat*en?*
> What *have* the boys eat*en?*
> The boys *have* not eat*en.*
> *Have*n't the boys eat*en?*

Shifting stress does not break the link

> The BOYS *have* eat*en.*
> The boys *HAVE* eat*en.*
> The boys *have* EAT*en.*

Larger, more complete structures do not break the link.

> The boys who *have* eat*en* are my brothers.
> My brothers are the boys who *have* eat*en.*
> The boys *have,* with little difficulty, eat*en* all the cake.

There is, quite obviously, some underlying connection between the auxiliary *have* and then *-en* morpheme in English sentences. When the auxiliary *have* comes into a kernel sentence it brings along a past participle morpheme. The past participle morpheme does not enter a kernel sentence unless escorted by the auxiliary *have*.

The same underlying relationship can be shown to exist between the auxiliary *be* and the present participle morpheme *-ing*. They come into kernel sentences together; neither comes in without the other.

For overall simplicity in our description of the grammar of English, it is best to make this fundamental point as early as possible. The underlying structure will bob to the surface in transform after transform with a variety of appearances on the surface, but each will reinforce the validity of our assumption that it lies below the surface in all kernel sentences.

It is possible to see the *have* + *-en* and *be* + *-ing* combinations in the auxiliary as single forms that simply have discontinuous elements. Other underlying relationships existing in the English language are not so easily pinned together. There are, for example, the relationships existing between the italicized parts of the sentences below.

> *Ruth read* the *book.*
> The *book* was *read* by *Ruth.*
> *Ruth* relaxed on Tuesday afternoon and *read* the *book.*
> *Ruth* bought the *book* on Monday and *read* it on Tuesday.
> *Ruth read* the play and the *book* on Tuesday.

These sentence parts, like the elements of the auxiliary, do not always turn up in the same order in the surface appearance of English sentences but, again like the auxiliary elements, represent similar relationships in each sentence. Consideration of the ways that these relationships are handled throughout the grammar of English both verifies the fact that they do exist beneath the surface and brings order to an explanation of the surface diversity.

We have referred to the way a sentence is spoken by a native speaker as the *surface structure* of that sentence. The underlying relationships are sometimes referred to as *deep structure*. Others use the terms *outer* and *inner structure*. While the deep structure is not always readily apparent in the spoken or written sentences of our language, it is stored in the intuition of the native speaker and influences both the way that he forms the sentences he speaks or writes and his understanding of those spoken or written by others.

13

SINGLE-BASE TRANSFORMATION

Transformations may, as the Affix Transformation does, rearrange elements in a string of symbols. They may do other things as well. They may order the addition of certain elements; they may order the deletion of certain elements; and they may order the combination of certain types of terminal strings.

The transformational rule always states the appearance of the string—the sequence of symbols—to the left of the double-barred arrow, ⇒, and then the changed or transformed string of symbols ordered by the rule to the right of the arrow.

Some transformational rules are *obligatory*. They must always be applied in order to produce a grammatical sentence. The Affix Transformation rule is one of these. PS Rule 4 states that A—which includes t, or tense—is a part of every verb phrase of every kernel sentence in English. In order to affix tense to the proper element in whatever follows, the Affix Transformation must be applied in the process of deriving any kernel sentence. It is an obligatory rule.

Other rules are called *optional* rules. They *may* be applied to kernel sentence terminal strings to produce other sentences in the language. A simple optional transformation is one that allows for the mobility of some English adverbs. For example, the terminal string NP   V   Av-m may be rearranged by the simple transformational rule

$$\text{NP} \quad \text{V} \quad \text{Av-m} \Rightarrow \text{NP} \quad \text{Av-m} \quad \text{V}$$

Sentences such as

The boys ate slowly.
The girls became friendly reluctantly.

may be transformed into

The boys slowly ate.
The girls reluctantly became friendly.

The shifting of the adverb of manner in these sentences is a possible transformation, not a mandatory one. The rule is an optional rule.
As stated earlier, transformation may do any of the following:

1. It may rearrange elements in a string.
2. It may add elements to a string.
3. It may delete elements from a string.
4. It may combine strings.

When any of the first three processes—or any combination of the three —is applied to a single terminal string of symbols, the transformation is called a *single-base transformation*. When strings are combined, the process is referred to as a *double-base transformation*. Double-base transformation is slightly more complex, as might be expected. Therefore, we will deal first with the simplest, most common types of single-base transformations.

The Yes/No Question Transformation

One of the most frequently used types of single-base transformation in English is that which produces yes/no questions. This means simply questions that may be answered either "Yes" or "No."
Once more, the choice of auxiliary elements is most important. The details of the Yes/No Question Transformation depend on which of the optional auxiliary elements have been chosen. We will deal with them one by one. Lexical substitutions have been included in square brackets beneath the terminal strings as an aid to understanding the strings of symbols and the transformations that are made.
If a modal is part of the auxiliary, the string of symbols might look like any of the following examples:

1. NP   t   M   have   -en   be   -ing V_T NP
   [He past can have -en be -ing eat cookies.]

2. NP   t   M   be -ing V_I
[He pres will be -ing go.]

3. NP   t   M V_c Aj
[He pres must become friendly.]

The Yes/No Question Transformation deals with the first three elements in the string and so it begins

$$NP \quad t \quad M \quad X$$

with X taking the place of *whatever follows the modal*. Whatever follows the modal need not be itemized because it will not be changed in any way. In forming a yes/no question, only the first three elements are rearranged. They are rearranged, or transformed, in this way:

$$NP \quad t \quad M \quad X \Rightarrow t \quad M \quad NP \quad X$$

Applying this transformation to the example strings above results in

1. <u>NP   t   M</u> have -en be -ing V_T NP
[He past can have -en be -ing eat cookies.]

<u>t   M   NP</u> have -en be -ing V_T NP
[past can he have -en be -ing eat cookies.]

If we apply the Affix Transformation rule to each string, the lexical substitutions we have chosen become:

Kernel sentence: *He could have been eating cookies.*
Yes/no question: *Could he have been eating cookies?*

2. <u>NP   t   M</u> be -ing V_I
[He pres will be -ing go.]

<u>t   M   NP</u> be -ing V_I
[pres will he be -ing go.]

If we apply the Affix Transformation rule as before, the lexical substitutions we have chosen become:

Kernel sentence: *He will be going.*
Yes/no question: *Will he be going?*

3. <u>NP   t   M</u> V_c Aj
[He pres must become friendly.]

<u>t   M   NP</u>   V$_c$ Aj
[pres must he become friendly.]

If we apply the Affix Transformation rule as before, the lexical substitutions we have chosen become:

Kernel sentence: *He must become friendly.*
Yes/no question: *Must he become friendly?*

If a modal does not appear in the string, then the next element—whether *have* or *be*—becomes the element shifted with the tense morpheme to form yes/no questions. The transformational rule notations are

NP t have X $\Rightarrow$ t have NP X
NP t be   X $\Rightarrow$ t be   NP X

Examples of the application of the changes ordered here are

4. <u>NP   t   have</u> -en V$_1$ Av-m
   [He pres have -en drive carefully.]

     <u>t have NP</u> -en V$_1$ Av-m
   [pres have he -en drive carefully.]

If we apply the Affix Transformation rule as before, the lexical substitutions we have chosen become:

Kernel sentence: *He has driven carefully.*
Yes/no question: *Has he driven carefully?*

5. <u>NP t be</u> -ing V$_c$ Aj
   [He past be -ing become friendly.]

    <u>t be NP</u> -ing V$_c$ Aj
   [past be he -ing become friendly.]

If we apply the Affix Transformation rule as before, the lexical substitutions we have chosen become:

Kernel sentence: *He was becoming friendly.*
Yes/no question: *Was he becoming friendly?*

A fourth possibility is that none of the auxiliary forms has been chosen except for the mandatory tense. If this is the case, the yes/no question transformation rule varies depending upon whether the main verb structure is headed by the category *be* or some other verb. The category *be* will make the shift with the tense morpheme; other verbs will not. As noted earlier, there are many ways in which the verb *be* behaves that are unlike the ways of all other verbs. The transformational notations covering those strings in which no other auxiliary form except the tense morpheme appears are these:

$$\text{NP} \quad t \quad be \quad \text{X} \Rightarrow t \quad be \quad \text{NP} \quad \text{X}$$
$$\text{NP} \quad t \quad \text{V} \quad \text{X} \Rightarrow t \quad \text{NP} \quad \text{V} \quad \text{X}$$

Examples of how *be* behaves are the following strings, their transforms and some lexical substitutions:

6. <u>NP   t   *be*</u>   Aj
    [He   past   be   tall.]
    <u>t   *be*   NP</u>   Aj
    [past   be   he   tall.]

If we apply the Affix Transformation rule as before, the lexical substitutions we have chosen become:

    Kernel sentence: *He was tall.*
    Yes/no question: *Was he tall?*

An example of how other verbs behave is shown by the following strings and lexical substitutions:

7. <u>NP   t V_T</u>   NP
    [He   past   eat   the cookies.]
    <u>t   NP V_T</u>   NP
    [past   he   eat   the cookies.]

It is now impossible to apply the Affix Transformation rule because the *Af* form, tense, is not followed by a *v* form with which it may be switched. Another obligatory rule becomes necessary. This rule, $t \Rightarrow do\ t$, changes an isolated tense morpheme into do-plus-tense. Application of this rule in the case of the sentence above results in the following lexical strings:

    Kernel sentence: *He ate the cookies.*
    Yes/no question: *Did he eat the cookies?*

The complete Yes/No Question Transformation rule then requires the following notations:

NP	t	M	X$\Rightarrow$t	M	NP	X
NP	t	have	X$\Rightarrow$t	have	NP	X
NP	t	be	X$\Rightarrow$t	be	NP	X
NP	t	*be*	X$\Rightarrow$t	*be*	NP	X
NP	t	V	X$\Rightarrow$t	NP	V	X

and the Do Transformation rule: t $\Rightarrow$ *do*   t

It may seem unnecessary to list the auxiliary *be* separately from the verb *be* but it is best to keep this distinction clearly in mind and the extra line of notation is worthwhile if it helps to accomplish this.

Consideration should be given to the other auxiliary form, *have,* which has a twin, *have,* in the ranks of the full verbs. In formal usage *have* will make the shift with the tense morpheme so that the kernel sentence "He has a car." can become the yes/no question "Has he a car?" This peculiarity, probably based on the similarity of the verb to the auxiliary form, would have to be noted in a highly detailed description of English syntax. It has not been accounted for here for two reasons. First, the more common usage follows the rule above. English speakers form yes/no questions like "Does he have a car?" to the almost total exclusion of questions like "Has he a car?" Second, other verbs of the *have* type, such as *weigh* and *cost,* operate as other verbs do in yes/no questions. English speakers do not say "Weighs it ten pounds?" or "Costs it six dollars?"

OTHER SINGLE-BASE TRANSFORMATIONS

Two other single-base transformations are very similar to the Yes/No Question Transformation in that their application depends upon the elements of the auxiliary that appear in the kernel sentence to be transformed. These two transformations are the Negative Transformation and the Reaffirmation Transformation.

The Negative Transformation

Any kernel sentence in English may be transformed into a negative sentence in English with the addition of a single word, *not.* The point at which this word may be added to the kernel string is determined by the auxiliary elements that appear in the kernel sentence being transformed.

As with the Yes/No Question Transformation, changes ordered by the Negative Transformation affect only the first few items in the kernel string. These, together with an X standing in for all the items that follow, are specified to the left of the double-barred transformation arrow. To the right of the arrow, these items appear with the form *not* inserted in the position required by the rules of English grammar. Several lines of notation are needed to account for sentences representing alternatives possible in the auxiliary.

The complete Negative Transformation is:

$$
\begin{array}{llllllll}
\text{NP} & \text{t} & \text{M} & \text{X} \Rightarrow \text{NP} & \text{t} & \text{M} & not & \text{X} \\
\text{NP} & \text{t} & \text{have} & \text{X} \Rightarrow \text{NP} & \text{t} & \text{have} & not & \text{X} \\
\text{NP} & \text{t} & \text{be} & \text{X} \Rightarrow \text{NP} & \text{t} & \text{be} & not & \text{X} \\
\text{NP} & \text{t} & \textit{be} & \text{X} \Rightarrow \text{NP} & \text{t} & \textit{be} & not & \text{X} \\
\text{NP} & \text{t} & \text{V} & \text{X} \Rightarrow \text{NP} & \text{t} & not & \text{V} & \text{X} \\
\end{array}
$$

The isolated tense morpheme in the last line of the transformation dictates use of the Do Transformation: $\text{t} \Rightarrow do \quad \text{t}$

Each of the kernel sentences below represents a different choice of auxiliary elements. Each requires application of a different line of the Negative Transformation above. The negative sentence examples are the result of applying the appropriate line of the transformation. The last requires the Do Transformation as well.

Kernel Sentences	*Negative Sentences*
Nancy may win the medal.	Nancy may not win the medal.
David had chosen the book.	David had not chosen the book.
Carolyn is writing a poem.	Carolyn is not writing a poem.
Martha is my friend.	Martha is not my friend.
Pat plays basketball.	Pat does not play basketball.

The rules will, of course, apply to any kernel sentence to produce a negative sentence. They will generate as many negative sentences as the PS rules will produce kernel strings.

The entire left half of the set of rules for the Negative Transformation is exactly the same as the left half of the set of rules for the Yes/No Question Transformation for the simple reason that the same items in kernel strings are involved in transformations forming yes/no questions and negative sentences.

Other similarities in the two transformations are (1) that the full verb *be* operates in the same way that the auxiliary *be* operates; (2) that the full verb *have* generally does not operate as its auxiliary twin, *have,* operates but follows the same procedure that other full verbs follow; and (3) that, in the case of kernel sentences where no auxiliary elements are chosen other than the mandatory *tense,* the tense morpheme becomes isolated in the transformed string and the Do Transformation becomes obligatory.

The Reaffirmation Transformation

Another transformation that follows the same general pattern of the Yes/No Question and Negative Transformations, is the Reaffirmation Transformation. The result of this transformation is readily apparent in the stress patterns of spoken English but can only be indicated in written language by underlining or using some other device for indicating heavy stress on a single word.

All kernel sentences are affirmative. Laying extra stress at a given point in such a sentence reinforces this affirmative quality of the sentence. For example, the sentence "You can do it." may be given an extra measure of insistence with the addition of extra stress on the word *can,* "You *can* do it."

This extra measure of affirmation, called *reaffirmation,* may be added to any kernel sentence in English. The addition in each case is a matter of stress. The point at which stress is added to a kernel sentence to produce reaffirmation is determined by the auxiliary elements that appear in the kernel sentence to be transformed.

The entire left half of the set of rules that make up the Reaffirmation Transformation is identical to those of the Yes/No Question and Negative Transformations. The added element of stress will be symbolized here by the abbreviation *Reaf.*

NP	t	M	X	$\Rightarrow$	NP	t	M	Reaf	X
NP	t	have	X	$\Rightarrow$	NP	t	have	Reaf	X
NP	t	be	X	$\Rightarrow$	NP	t	be	Reaf	X
NP	t	*be*	X	$\Rightarrow$	NP	t	*be*	Reaf	X
NP	t	V	X	$\Rightarrow$	NP	t	Reaf	V	X

The isolated tense morpheme in the last line of the transformation dictates use of the Do Transformation: t $\Rightarrow$ *do*   t

Each of the kernel sentences below represents a different choice of auxiliary elements. Each requires application of a different line of the Reaffirmation Transformation above. The transformed sentences—with the reaffirmation stress indicated by italicization—are the result of applying the appropriate line of the transformation. The last requires use of the Do Transformation as well.

Kernel Sentences	*Reaf Sentences*
They can learn the music.	They *can* learn the music.
Kate has succeeded.	Kate *has* succeeded.
They are collecting stamps.	They *are* collecting stamps.
Danny is here.	Danny *is* here.
She studied for the test.	She *did* study for the test.

For purposes of simplicity, we have used no kernel sentence examples that include more than one optional auxiliary element. Choices of more than one optional element will not affect application of the rules. The X of the transformational rules includes everything that follows the affected elements of the kernel sentence. The following terminal strings are examples:

    1. *The girl past can be -ing help her friend.*
        NP   t   M   X

    2. *The girl ·past shall have -en be -ing help her friend.*
        NP   t   M   X

    3. *The girl pres have en be -ing help her friend.*
        NP   t   have   X

Application of the Yes/No Question Transformation and the Affix Transformation to each of the kernel sentences above will produce:

    1. Could the girl be helping her friend?
    2. Should the girl have been helping her friend?
    3. Has the girl been helping her friend?

Application of the Negative Transformation and the Affix Transformation to each of the kernel sentence examples will produce:

    1. The girl could not be helping her friend.
    2. The girl should not have been helping her friend.
    3. The girl has not been helping her friend.

Application of the Reaffirmation Transformation and the Affix Transformation to each of the kernel sentence examples will produce:

    1. The girl *could* be helping her friend.
    2. The girl *should* have been helping her friend.
    3. The girl *has* been helping her friend.

The orderly nature of these three transformations demonstrates once again the systematic nature of the rules of English grammar. This system is not the creation of generative grammar theory; it is a part of the grammar of the English language. Transformational-generative theory attempts to describe that system in a concise and effective way.

The Passive Transformation

The single-base transformations that we have dealt with to this point may apply to all kernel sentences in English. Other transformations may have limited application. That is, they may not be applied to all kernel sentences. Such limitations are written into the transformational rules. There is, for example, the Passive Transformation.

The Passive Transformation may be written

$$NP_1 \quad A \quad V_t \quad NP_2 \Rightarrow NP_2 \quad A \quad be \quad \text{-en} \quad V_T \quad (by \ NP_1)$$

The subscript numbers simply establish a label for each noun phrase of the kernel sentence. Location in the PS rules and, therefore, in the terminal strings of kernel sentences, establishes the function of various types of structures in kernel sentences. The parenthesis enclosing the final elements of the transformed string indicates that these elements are optional, that is, they may or may not be deleted in the passive sentence. For example:

Jack has eaten the cake. ⇒   The cake has been eaten by Jack.
                              or The cake has been eaten.

The fact that a V_T is specified in the string to the left of the arrow eliminates the possibility of the transformation being applied to sentences such as "The boy is my brother," "The baby laughed," or "The man became a doctor." None of these sentences contains a V_T and none can be transformed into a passive sentence.

Most kernel sentences containing transitive verbs can be transformed into passive sentences by means of the changes and additions ordered by the transformational rule above. Examples are:

Alice cut the flowers.   ⇒ The flowers were cut by Alice.

The child threw the ball.   ⇒ The ball was thrown by the child.

The firemen extinguished the blaze. ⇒ The blaze was extinguished by the firemen.

A few kernel sentences containing transitive verbs show peculiarities that block the Passive Transformation. Examples are "George broke his arm," and "The clock struck midnight." Precise definition of these peculiarities would be contained in a full description of the rules of English grammar.

Among other things, this would involve a greater variety of noun and verb categories and consideration of semantic relationships. We will return to the problem of establishing more precise definitions of this type when we turn to consideration of the noun phrase. For the present we will keep our rules as simple as possible and allow for their lack of precision by saying that *almost all* the kernel sentences in English that contain a transitive verb may be transformed into passive sentences by application of the Passive Transformation given above.

The THERE Transformation

Another frequently used single-base transformation that has limited application is one involving use of the function word *there* as a kind of temporary subject. Again, restrictions as to the use of the transformation are written into that part of the transformation to the left of the arrow:

$$D \quad N \quad A \quad be \quad \text{Adv-p} \Rightarrow There \quad A \quad be \quad D \quad N \quad \text{Adv-p}$$

A kernel sentence such as "The boy was in the treehouse" may be transformed into "There was a boy in the treehouse" by use of this transformation. Further elaboration of the rule would allow for other uses of this function word that result in such sentences as

There are reasons for his self-assurance.
There were three major factors involved.
There were some men repairing the roof.

These, like the rules allowing for greater precision in the Passive Transformation, are a matter of defining word categories and functional relationships in greater detail.

The few single-base transformations presented here are only samples of the workings of this type of transformation. English grammar includes a large and quite varied number of such transformations. Several, such as the transformations that produce questions beginning with *who, why, what, where,* and *how,* are as frequently used as those presented here.

English has extremely flexible and creative grammatical rules. Description of these rules, even with the compact formulas of transformational-generative theory, is quite a long and involved undertaking.

14

THE NOUN PHRASE

Because generative grammar theory is still in its developmental stage, several aspects of the theory are still in tentative form. This is no reason to suppose that the entire theory should be left in the laboratory until every detail is perfected. It would be just as sensible to suppose that we should ignore the whole field of astronomy until someone invents a telescope that will enable man to see the limits of the universe. There is reason, however, for the classroom teacher to proceed with some caution in adapting the theories of generative grammarians to classroom use.

It must be remembered that the generative grammarian is not developing a theory in a vacuum. He deals with something that already exists—language. He seeks to explain the phenomena of language in as orderly, simple and concise a manner as possible; he does not seek to "whip it into shape." The problem is not one of developing a system. The system is already there—in the intuition of the speakers of the language. The task he has set for himself is one of discovering how the system works and bringing order to his description of what he discovers.

The classroom teacher does not need to possess a detailed knowledge of cybernetics, advanced mathematics, psycholinguistics, analytic philosophy, and so on—although linguistic scholars often must have such a background—to understand and make use of some of the theory. The teacher does not need to follow every detail of the efforts of linguistic scholars at the frontiers of their research. Much has already been done; much has been shown to pass empirical test; much has been subjected to that test which interests the teacher most vitally—use in the classroom. Results of these studies are things that the teacher should try to investigate and understand.

We have been investigating some of the basics of generative grammar theory. These basics represent the parts of the theory that are universally accepted by generative grammarians. Among these are: first, that symbolic representation of categories and relationships is a useful device for concise description of the syntax of a language; second, that a combination of phrase structure rules and transformational rules is more effective than phrase structure rules alone in dealing with the tremendous variety and creativity of language; and, third, that preliminary categorization may be based on analysis of the environments in which various elements may appear. Some of this is demonstrated by the use of the simple phrase structure and transformational rules already covered.

In dealing with the phrase structure and transformational rules of the noun phrase, it is possible to strengthen our grasp of the points already covered and to approach some of the more recent developments in the overall theory. We can also begin to see some of the areas toward which generative research scholars are, at the moment, directing their efforts.

The noun phrase—the NP of our first rewrite rule, as well as the NP's that serve as part of the environment of some verb categories—is a category that demands careful and detailed subcategorization. The noun phrase of English is a tremendously rich and creative category. A consideration of some of the simpler phrase structure rules devoted to its description will help to demonstrate this. These PS rule numbers will not follow those used earlier, because we are, in effect, going back to fill in some of the detail omitted earlier.

PS Rule 1 $S \rightarrow NP \quad VP$

PS Rule 2 $NP \rightarrow \begin{Bmatrix} Prop \ N \\ Pron \\ D \quad N \end{Bmatrix} \ (S)$

PS Rule 3 $D \rightarrow (PreDet \quad of) \begin{Bmatrix} Art \\ Dem \end{Bmatrix} (Post \ D)$

RS Rule 4 $Art \rightarrow \begin{Bmatrix} Def \\ Indef \end{Bmatrix}$

PS Rule 5 $Post \ D \rightarrow num$

PS Rule 6 $num \rightarrow \begin{Bmatrix} card \\ ord \\ ord \quad card \end{Bmatrix}$

Symbols Used:

S	sentence	Art	article
NP	noun phrase	of	the word *of*
VP	verb phrase	Dem	demonstrative
Prop N	proper noun	Post D	post determiner
Pron	pronoun	Def	definite
D	determiner	Indef	indefinite
N	noun	num	number
PreDet	predeterminer	card	cardinal
		ord	ordinal

Pronouns are words like *you, he, they, we, someone, anything, everyone, nobody,* and *something;* predeterminers are words like *all, some,* and *each;* the definite article is *the;* indefinite articles are *a, an,* and a Ø form; demonstratives are *this, these, that,* and *those;* cardinal numbers are *one, two, three,* and so on; ordinal numbers are *first, second, third,* and so on.

Before we take up PS Rule 2, it will be well to consider the determiner system of English as a unit. Rules 3–6 are all concerned with the determiner system—one of the most complex areas of the English language. It hardly seems necessary to point out that this complexity was invented by speakers of English, not generative grammarians! Placing the rewrite rules for the determiner system in another relation to each other may help to clarify them somewhat.

$$3 \;\; D \rightarrow (\text{PreDet} + \text{of}) \begin{Bmatrix} \text{Art} \\ \text{Dem} \end{Bmatrix} \qquad (\text{Post D})$$

$$4 \;\; \text{Art} \rightarrow \begin{Bmatrix} \text{Def} \\ \text{Indef} \end{Bmatrix} \qquad 5 \;\; \text{Post D} \rightarrow \text{num}$$

$$6 \;\; \text{num} \rightarrow \begin{Bmatrix} \text{card} \\ \text{ord} \\ \text{ord} \quad \text{card} \end{Bmatrix}$$

These rules do not account for all of the possible combinations in the English determiner system. Even more detail would be necessary to do so, but the analysis above demonstrates the underlying order of a system that results in such apparently diverse combinations as:

Some of these four boys . . .
Few of the girls . . .
The boys . . .
Most of this country . . .

Few of us . . .
Each of the first six boys . . .
Those girls . . .

It is not surprising that speakers of other languages find the English determiner system one of the most difficult areas of the language to master.

Returning to PS Rule 2, we can begin to consider some of the problems of categorizing English nouns. In order to define the subcategories of the category NP, some thought must be given to those nouns which do not work with a determiner as well as those that do. The generative grammarian simply notes that this distinction exists:

$$\text{PS Rule 2 NP} \rightarrow \left\{ \begin{matrix} \text{Prop N} \\ \text{Pron} \\ \text{D N} \end{matrix} \right\} \text{ (S)}$$

This rule sets apart those forms which do not work with determiners (proper nouns such as *Mrs. Brown, France, Mt. Hood,* and so on, and pronouns such as *he, she, somebody, anyone, everything,* and so on) from all other nouns in English.

There are many other considerations involved in rewriting the symbol N, which stands for all other nouns in English. All these nouns show number. Those characteristics which set apart types of nouns which regularly show either the singular or plural number must be recognized. These must be contrasted with those characteristics which mark nouns that are almost always singular. Some nouns are almost always singular because they involve a consideration of mass. These include such terms as *water* and *sand.* Others are almost always singular because they involve abstract qualities such as *truth* and *greed.* English speakers do not discuss two waters or two greeds with any regularity. There are, nevertheless, some contexts in which many mass nouns take the plural number quite easily—"the flood waters rose," "the sands of time," "we hold these truths," and so on. Other problems of number involve purely idiomatic usage, as with:

The army was called out to deal with the emergency.
The police were called out to deal with the emergency.

The verbs in the example sentences indicate that the speaker of English considers *army* to be a singular term, but *police* a plural one. Establishing categories that will allow for these types of differences in detail involves highly complex PS Rules.

All of this detail is a part of the grammatical system of English.

The rules that include this detail represent an analysis of the more complex underlying system that catalogues, for the speaker of English, such information as which words take a plural morpheme and when, which nouns work with certain verb categories, which nouns may serve as objects of certain verbs, and so on.

A more recent method of dealing with the subcategorization of forms recognizes the fact that the division between syntax and semantics is not a clearly defined one. The lexicon, therefore, bears more of the burden of classification of specific items. The information formerly contained in such rewrite rules as "$V_L \rightarrow$ *seem, become, remain . . .*" is incorporated into the more elaborate lexicon.

Some generative grammarians make use of special sets of rules to handle the sorting of nouns and verbs. These sorting operations are sometimes quite complex depending upon how precise the grammarian hopes to make his final categories. The subcategorization that follows will be be a comparatively simple one designed simply to suggest the kinds of sorting involved. The rules will be given in the form of rewrite rules in order to keep them consistent with the method used for earlier PS rules.

$$N \rightarrow \begin{Bmatrix} \text{D} \quad \text{common noun} \\ \text{proper noun} \\ \text{pronoun} \end{Bmatrix}$$

$$\text{common noun} \rightarrow \begin{Bmatrix} \text{N+count} \begin{Bmatrix} z_1 \\ \emptyset \end{Bmatrix} \\ \text{N−count} \end{Bmatrix}$$

$$\text{N+count} \rightarrow \begin{Bmatrix} \text{N+animate} \\ \text{N−animate} \end{Bmatrix}$$

$$\text{N+animate} \rightarrow \begin{Bmatrix} \text{N+human} \\ \text{N−human} \end{Bmatrix}$$

$$\text{N−count} \rightarrow \begin{Bmatrix} \text{N+abstract} \\ \text{N−abstract} \end{Bmatrix}$$

The step-by-step sorting operation is this:

$$N \rightarrow \begin{Bmatrix} \text{D} \quad \text{common noun} \\ \text{proper noun} \\ \text{pronoun} \end{Bmatrix}$$

This rule is included to point up the fact that the nouns that are subdivided below are *common nouns*. No proper nouns or pronouns are included.

$$\text{common noun} \rightarrow \left\{ \begin{array}{l} \text{N+count} \left\{ \begin{array}{l} z_1 \\ \emptyset \end{array} \right\} \\ \text{N−count} \end{array} \right\}$$

common nouns
    may be divided into   count nouns such as *boy, door, cat, book*. Most have both singular and plural forms.

        and   noncount or mass nouns such as *air, mush, integrity*

$$\text{N+count} \rightarrow \left\{ \begin{array}{l} \text{N+animate} \\ \text{N−animate} \end{array} \right\}$$

count nouns
    may be divided into   animate nouns such as *boy, cat, man, squirrel*

        and   inanimate nouns such as *stone, door, house, book*

$$\text{N+animate} \rightarrow \left\{ \begin{array}{l} \text{N+human} \\ \text{N−human} \end{array} \right\}$$

animate nouns
    may be divided into   human nouns such as *man, boy, child*
        and   nonhuman nouns such as *cat, squirrel, dog, mouse*

$$\text{N−count} \rightarrow \left\{ \begin{array}{l} \text{N+abstract} \\ \text{N−abstract} \end{array} \right\}$$

noncount nouns
    may be divided into   abstract nouns such as *integrity, cowardice, courage*
        and   nonabstract or concrete nouns such as *air, mush, dust*

Other means of stating the sorting operations above are possible, the simplest being a separate chart of subcategories of nouns. English verbs, too, may be sorted into various subcategories by one means or another. Consideration may then be given to which types of nouns function with which types of verbs and what sorts of functional relationships they may enter into.

The important point is that such subcategorization, regardless of how it is handled, refines the number and kinds of combinations possible in sentences. These rules reduce the possibility of such nonsense sentences as "The news amazed the door." and "The squirrel smoked a cigar."

If rules such as those above were incorporated into the PS rules, they would transfer to the tree diagrams. For example, see the diagram below.

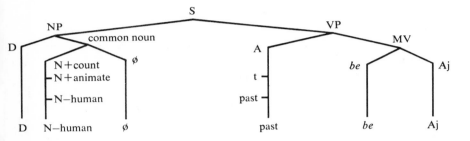

One of the entries in the lexicon might read:

cat, /kæt/, common noun, N+count, N+animate, N−human, sing/pl

Such an entry contrasts the form *cat* with noncount or mass nouns, with inanimate nouns, with human nouns. It also includes morphographemic information, that is, the symbols representing the written form of the word; morphophonemic information, that is, a phonemic transcription of the sounds of the spoken form; and the information that this form has both a singular and a plural form in contrast to those nouns which have only a singular or only a plural form—*music, measles, mathematics, news,* and so on.

Further elaboration in the lexicon entry for the form *cat* would include certain environmental restrictions. These would detail the types of verbs with which *cat* might work and the types of complements and objects it might take. These rules are often called *selectional rules.* Such an elaboration would border on, or actually overlap, a semantic definition. A complete lexicon might, in fact, include a semantic definition.

Such a detailed lexicon is not so far removed from the traditional dictionary. Its difference from the traditional dictionary is in the unity of the symbols used in the lexicon entries and the symbols used in the PS rules. The PS rules establish grammatical categories; the Lexicon establishes classification of *forms* into the categories. The symbols of both allow for the interlocking of such procedures, which must be a part of the intuitive knowledge of the native speaker of the language.

Teachers of English who have made it their business to teach grammatical structure (by whatever means), spelling, standard pronunciation, and vocabulary should find no real surprises in this approach to the problems of analyzing the grammar of the English language. They should be able to find, in generative grammar theory, a more effective means of relating these more or less isolated activities to each other. Fragmenting the study of language is sometimes unavoidable in the context of the English classroom. Building connecting links between the fragments can and should be the aim of every language teacher. An overall view of the tremendous complexity of the language that we use daily should not be a forbidding thing to teacher or student. The ability to use and understand complex language systems sets man apart from all other life forms, and the ability to use these systems in endlessly creative and imaginative ways sets him apart from even the most staggeringly complex machines. Language is, in this light, the most humanistic of studies.

Subcategorization and classification procedures dealing with complex sets of syntactic features are more complicated than the categorizing procedures of our preliminary PS rules. The simplified PS rules listed for demonstrating basic sentence types were generalizations. Like other generalizations, they have their limitations. Nevertheless, to say that we must never make generalizations—particularly in dealing with a subject as complex as English grammar—is to say that we must never discuss the subject at all.

The rewrite rules may be seen as representing levels of structure. The most basic level is that which says that all kernel sentences are made up of an NP and a VP. The next level, as far as the noun phrase is concerned, separates the D, or determiner, forms from the N, or other noun phrase forms. In the verb phrase, succeeding levels show the separation of the VP into auxiliary forms and the rest of the main verb structure and so on. A nonsense sentence that follows the grammatical structure of English as described by the rules for these basic levels may very well violate the grammatical structure imposed by rules added at later levels. For example, we earlier made arbitrary lexical substitutions for the category symbols of the terminal strings derived from a set of simplified phrase structure rules. Clearly we made choices that were not dictated *in detail* by those PS rules. Lexical substitution for the terminal string D N past V_T D N Av-m might very well be

"The boys ate the cookies eagerly." It might also be "A boy ate the city eagerly," "The cookies ate the city eagerly," or even "The noise frightened the wall terribly." Such sentences do not violate the grammatical structure described by our generalized rules. They are simply nonsense sentences which follow the most basic grammatical patterns of English. Grammatical sentences in English may be either sensible or nonsense just as they may be either true or false.

These nonsense sentences would violate the structure imposed by more detailed subcategorizations. That is, they would be ungrammatical at later levels because of the added restrictions on types of lexical substitutions that would be allowed. On the other hand, strings of words such as "city eagerly the ate boy" and "frightened wall the terribly noise the" violate even the most basic levels of structure and are, therefore, ungrammatical in any sense.

Establishment of levels of structure or levels of grammaticality enables the grammarian or teacher a means of approaching the workings of English grammar. The study of basic levels of structure—always with the stipulation that more complex levels do exist—allows for generalization in the study of grammatical patterning. This generalization is helpful in allowing for simpler rules for larger structures; it is harmful only if the grammarian, teacher, or student forgets the fact that it *is* generalization. Further levels of complexity may then be added to the basic levels with each adding a more thorough grasp of the complexity of the grammatical code shared by speakers and hearers of the language.

15

DOUBLE-BASE TRANSFORMATION

In order to study the processes of double-base transformation, it is helpful to begin with simple strings dealing only with the most basic levels of structure. We must do some generalizing about the NP of English sentences by dispensing with the detail of the determiner system and the subcategories of nouns so that we may concentrate on the last part of our NP rewrite rule:

$$\text{PS Rule 2} \quad \text{NP} \rightarrow \left\{ \begin{array}{l} \text{Prop N} \\ \text{Pron} \\ \text{D} \quad \text{N} \end{array} \right\} \text{ (S)}$$

The rule says that any noun phrase structure may or may not be followed by a sentence. When such a sentence does follow a noun phrase structure, it must, obviously, be embedded in the sentence of which the NP is a part.

For example, see the diagram on page 177.

Embedding the sentence in square brackets into the main sentence involves changing some elements—the determiner and noun of the sentence to be embedded—and the changing of elements is among the processes assigned to the transformational rules. In this case the transformational rule must deal with two strings of symbols—that of the main sentence and that of the sentence to be embedded. Rules for this type of operation are called *double-base transformations*. The main sentence is usually referred to as the *matrix sentence*. This is a very precise descriptive term; the dictionary definition of *matrix* is "that which gives origin or form to a thing, or which serves to enclose it."

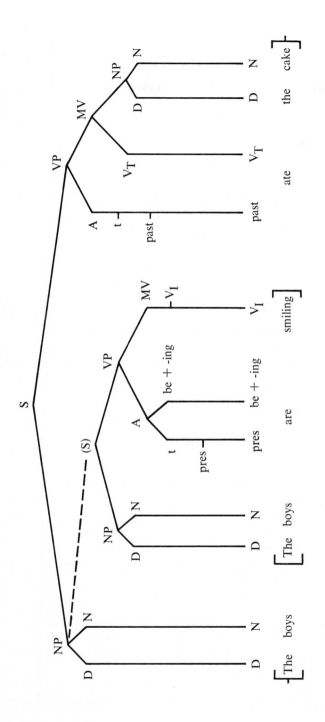

The sentence that must be embedded in the matrix sentence is some-times called the *constituent sentence* because it is a part of a larger structure, and sometimes called the *insert sentence* because that is what we propose to do with it.

The Relative-Clause Transformation

Before embedding of constituent sentences into matrix sentences can take place, certain relations must hold between the two sentences. These requirements are a part of the double-base transformational rules in each case.

In the example above, we must deal with the following strings of symbols and lexical items:

$$\text{Matrix:} \quad \text{D} \quad \text{N} \quad \text{pres } V_T \quad \text{D} \quad \text{N}$$
$$\text{-[The boys} \quad \text{ate} \quad \text{the cake]-}$$

$$\text{Constituent:} \quad \text{D} \quad \text{N} \quad \text{pres be} + \text{-ing } V_I$$
$$\text{[The boys} \quad \text{are} \quad \text{smiling]}$$

and the combination:

$$\text{D} \quad \text{N} \quad \text{D} \quad \text{N} \quad \text{pres be} + \text{-ing } V_I \quad \text{past } V_T \text{ D N}$$
$$\text{-[The boys} \quad \text{[The boys} \quad \text{are} \quad \text{smiling]} \quad \text{ate the cake]-}$$

The transformational rule that applies in this case might read:

$$\text{D} \quad \text{N}_{Mat} \quad \text{D} \quad \text{N}_{Con} \Rightarrow \text{D} \quad \text{N} \begin{Bmatrix} \text{who} \\ \text{which} \\ \text{that} \end{Bmatrix}$$

$$\text{where} \quad \text{N}_{Mat} = \text{N}_{Con}$$

This is the transformational rule for the relative clause. The re-quirement that the noun of the matrix sentence and the noun of the constituent sentence must be the same is expressed symbolically by the = sign. This part of the rule blocks embedding of the constituent sen-tence as a relative clause unless the two nouns are the same. The lexical substitutions we have chosen meet the requirements of the transforma-tional rule and we may now change the sequence of forms as ordered by the rule. We must make a choice of relative pronouns and, in this case, might choose either *who* or *that*. Choice of *who* results in the sentence "The boys who are smiling ate the cake."

Noun phrases in English sentences may always contain or include another sentence. The noun phrase that serves as a part of the main verb structure in the string D N past V_T D N, for example, is also subject to the rewrite rule

$$NP \rightarrow \begin{Bmatrix} \text{Prop N} \\ \text{I Pr} \\ \text{D \ N} \end{Bmatrix} (S)$$

If this optional sentence is added in the case of the noun phrase that is a part of the main verb structure in the matrix sentence above, the probable result is shown by the diagram on page 180.

Again the lexical substitutions chosen meet the requirements of the transformational rule for the relative clause. Application of the rule results in the sentence "The boys ate the cake that was here."

The inclusion of the symbol (S) in the rewrite rule for the NP of kernel sentences makes the rule *recursive*. It may be used again and again in succeeding NPs. The rule also demonstrates the interlocking of the phrase structure rules and transformational rules that has led generative grammarians to consider them parts of a single component—called the syntactic component—of a generative grammar of the English language. They further demonstrate the overall objective of generative grammar theory which is to describe the language in terms of the distributional regularities and systematic relationships of its parts.

OTHER DOUBLE-BASE TRANSFORMATIONS

The notation that any noun phrase in any kernel sentence may be followed by another complete sentence is useful in many ways. The transformational rule that allows for incorporation of the constituent sentence into the matrix sentence as a relative clause is only one of these.

The Adjective Transformation

Whenever the constituent sentence is of the type that we have labeled Sentence Pattern A, that is, when it may be symbolized *NP A be Aj,* a simple transformational rule allows for the embedding of the adjective of the constituent sentence into the noun phrase of the matrix sentence when the noun phrase of the constituent sentence is identical to the noun phrase of the matrix sentence.

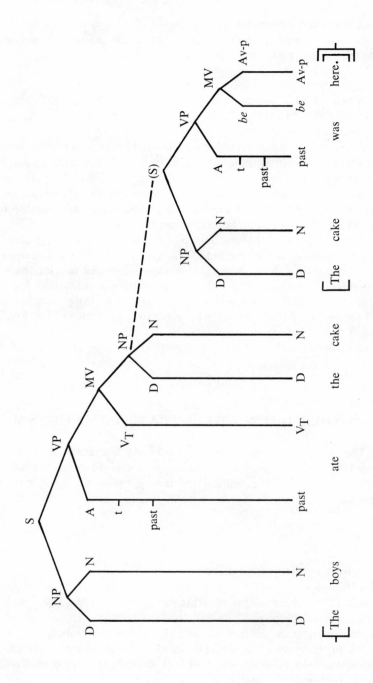

The transformational rule might read

$$D_{Mat} \quad N_{Mat} \quad D_{Con} \quad N_{Con} \quad be \quad Aj \quad VP_{Mat} \Rightarrow D_{Mat} \quad Aj \quad N_{Mat} \quad VP_{Mat}$$
where $D_{Mat} \quad N_{Mat} = D_{Con} \quad N_{Con}$

Sample lexical substitutions and brackets to indicate the matrix and constituent sentences will demonstrate the workings of the transformational rule.

$$D_{Mat} \quad N_{Mat} \quad D_{Con} \quad N_{Con} \quad be \quad Aj \quad VP_{Mat} \Rightarrow D_{Mat} \quad Aj \quad N_{Mat} \quad VP_{Mat}$$
-[The   boy [The   boy   is   tall.] smiled.]⊦⇒ The   tall   boy   smiled.

The Adjective Transformation is recursive and can, therefore, be used again and again. Results of multiple use are:

John bought a new red foreign car.
Rich blue velvet upholstery covered the beautiful antique chair.

The Appositive Transformation

A double-base transformational rule that results in a construction commonly called an appositive allows two noun phrases to stand side by side when the embedded sentence is of the NP *be* NP type and the noun phrases that function as subjects in both the matrix sentence and the constituent sentence are identical.

The transformational rule might read

$$NP_{Mat} \quad NP_{1\,Con} \quad be \quad NP_{2\,Con} \quad VP_{Mat} \Rightarrow NP_{Mat}, \quad NP_{2\,Con}, \quad VP_{Mat}$$
where $NP_{Mat} = NP_{1\,Con}$

Sample lexical substitutions and brackets to indicate the matrix and constituent sentences will demonstrate the workings of this transformational rule.

$$NP_{Mat} \quad NP_{1\,Con} \quad be \quad NP_{2\,Con} \quad VP_{Mat} \Rightarrow$$
-[Georgia [Georgia is the cheerleader.] sees all the games.]⊦ ⇒
$$NP_{Mat}, \quad NP_{2\,Con}, \quad VP_{Mat}$$
Georgia, the cheerleader, sees all the games.

Other examples of appositive constructions resulting from the embedding of constituents into matrix sentences according to the Appositive Transformation are:

George Washington, the first U.S. president, was a Virginian.

Sacramento, the capital of California, was their destination.

The uses of double-base transformation are only suggested by the examples given here. Kernel sentences in English may be combined in endless variation with sentences embedded in sentences which are, in turn, embedded in other sentences. The enormous range of syntactic possibilities in the English language, in combination with the richness and variety of the English vocabulary, gives to our language a truly remarkable versatility and creative scope.

PART FIVE

NOTES ON LINGUISTICS AND THE TEACHING OF ENGLISH LITERATURE AND COMPOSITION

16

LINGUISTICS AND THE TEACHING OF LITERATURE

Students in art appreciation classes are given some instruction in color, media, and design, and they are given summaries of historical development of style and technique before they are expected to deal with evaluation and appreciation of individual painters and their works. Students of music appreciation are given similar grounding in the tools available to composers and musicians, along with background on the development of various methods and styles of composition and techniques of performance, before they are expected to evaluate and appreciate the work of great composers and musicians. The findings of linguistic research can be used in much the same way to prepare students for a greater appreciation and understanding of the masterpieces of the literary art.

LANGUAGE SYSTEMS AND LITERATURE

PHONOLOGY   The sound system of English is of prime importance to poets; it should be equally important to those who read and study poetry. Teachers often point out such matters as rhyme scheme, masculine and feminine rhyme, assonance and alliteration, poetic meter, and so on, when teaching poetry. These are terms for some of the ways that a poet manipulates the sound system of his language. To begin such study without some knowledge of the sound system itself is like teaching an art student how to mix colors without preliminary study of the color wheel.

The vowel system of English cannot be sorted on the basis of English spelling, and linguistic research has effectively demonstrated that discussing the English vowel system in terms of long and short vowels is grossly misleading. These errors are compounded by the insistence upon teaching meter according to stressed and unstressed syllables. The stress patterns of English are more complex than that and the English-speaking student knows it. When he reads a line to himself, he is quite likely to hear more than the two degrees of stress that the metrical patterns insist on. The teacher can save a great deal of debate by admitting this difference and suggesting that unstressed syllables may vary slightly from light to very light and that stressed syllables may come in both heavy and very heavy varieties.

Students should be urged to read poetry aloud, it should be read to them and recordings of poetry readings should be played for them. Poetry is sound and can best be appreciated when it is presented as sound. Some musicians can read a musical score, "hearing" the music as they read, but most of the uninitiated need to have someone play the music before they can hear it. Teachers who assign a poem for homework sometimes mistakenly assume that the student will hear the poem as they read. Poetry, like music, needs a performer for the uninitiated. The teacher who does not read aloud effectively should make every effort to improve whatever skill he does possess with the aid of a tape recorder or some other type of training. In the meantime, excellent recordings are available.

It is often worthwhile to study a poem in three steps. First, a reading of the poem from beginning to end without comment allows the student an introduction to the piece as a whole. Second, the sound patterns—including the intonation pattern—can be taken apart line by line. Other aspects of poetry, imagery, simile, and metaphor, and other purely semantic considerations are a part of the process of taking the poem apart. Finally, the poem must be put back together and again read to the student from beginning to end. The final step is perhaps the most crucial and often the most easily overlooked. After a class has dismembered a poetic work in order to study the technique and style of the poet, they must hear it again in order to appreciate the effect of that technique and style.

Other writers also write for oral effect. Chief among these are playwrights. No playwright constructs his work to appeal to the eye. His creation, like that of the composer of music, is written to be performed for an audience. He writes, and revises, with oral sound constantly in mind. Great plays are paced so that scenes of great *oral* and emotional force alternate with scenes of lesser oral impact. The work is carefully orchestrated and must be heard or seen to be appreciated. Some of us "hear" these differences as we silently read a play; students often do not.

Writers of prose fiction and even simple exposition appeal to the inner ear as they write. Teachers sometimes make this point for their students by duplicating passages from novels or short stories in blank verse form. No words or grammatical constructions are changed—only the appearance of the passage on the page is rearranged to suggest the poetic form. Passages from Faulkner, Fitzgerald, and Thomas are particularly useful for this purpose.

MORPHOLOGY   The systematic word-building systems of English are so much a part of the unconscious knowledge of most teachers and their more verbally oriented students that teachers often miss the opportunity to give these tools to their slower students. Most teachers discuss the more commonly used prefixes and suffixes but usually by means of lists of these and their meanings. Such lists become only another tedious rote-learning chore for the student. It is possible to demonstrate the word-building capabilities of English much more fully if the teacher can bring herself to break vocabulary items with much more freedom and let the students explore the meanings for themselves. What, for example, have the *furn-* portions of *furnish, furniture,* and *furnishing* in common; or the *-flict* in *conflict* and *inflict* and even *affliction;* or the *-pose* portions of *compose, impose,* and *repose?* Students should not be allowed to consult a dictionary immediately but make some attempt to work the problem out—to exercise their own linguistic muscles—before consulting an authority. If they are able to arrive at reasonable explanations on their own, their knowledge of the word is success oriented. In any event, the definition is more likely to remain with them if they have wrestled with it for at least one round.

Most of these inquiries into the stems of compound and complex words will lead very naturally into some consideration of the shifting, changing nature of language. These considerations are, of course, most important when students are asked to read and try to understand a literary work representing an early period in English or American literature. Every teacher of Chaucer and Shakespeare recognizes this fact and teaches the literature accordingly; many who teach Brontë and Dickens and Twain do not.

Teachers too frequently attempt to fix blame on the students and their limited vocabulary; students fix blame on the author's word and syntactic pattern choice and say simply that they "don't like Dickens." To recognize that the language is used differently in our century is to avoid fixing blame and recognize a fact of life. Students can benefit from learning some of the terms and syntactic patterns more common to other centuries. For one thing, many of these are not completely obsolete and, for another, they are the key to a fuller appreciation of older literature. The dividing line is not distinct between those terms and usages that are virtually dead as far as Modern English is concerned and those that are worth learning as part of a more literate vocabulary. The former are usually footnoted, as with some of the terminology used by Shakespeare, and the student is not expected to make these a part of his vocabulary. Terminology from other, more recent works is often the basis for vocabulary studies. Students are asked to look up the words, memorize meanings, and use the words in sentences. Teachers who prepare such vocabulary lists should be very careful of their choice. Wise choices will lend themselves to the kind of vocabulary study suggested earlier and enable students to explore their language in more exciting and challenging ways than thumbing through a dictionary.

SYNTAX AND TRANSFORMATION Students sometimes assume that great writers simply sit down and let the words flow from their pen and that the words they read were the first flow of genius. They are often unaware of the laborious working out of phrases, modifiers, parallel and contrasting constructions and so on that represent that 90 percent of genius described as "perspiration."

Information about the patterns of the English language and the ways that the patterns may be transformed into an infinite variety of sentences can be used to demonstrate the alternatives available to any writer to express his ideas. A single complex sentence can be rewritten in several perfectly grammatical ways without changing any of the factual information, but each alternative will subtly shift emphasis and meaning. The writer has obviously made a choice among alternatives. The study of these choices is the study of stylistics.

Great writers show remarkable consistency in the choices that they make among the grammatical patterns of English. To see a consistency in the way that a writer manipulates the language is to identify his style. For students unused to identifying subtle differences in style, it is best to make sharp contrasts. It is often useful to compare the work of authors of similar background and literary period whose styles are quite different such as that of Hemingway and Fitzgerald. Another possibility is to compare the early work of a writer with that representing a much later stage of his career. Still another possibility is the study of a single work in which an author has varied his style for specific purpose as Alan Paton did in *Cry, the Beloved Country*.

DIALECT AND USAGE Similar in many ways to vocabulary and

syntactic differences that occur from one literary period to another, are contrastive terms and constructions related to geographical and social differences.

Many works of literature demand consideration of dialect differences. Among these are *Pygmalion, Huckleberry Finn,* all of the Faulkner novels and the Runyon short stories, and several of the most worthwhile examples of Negro literature that are only now being added to the reading lists in American schools.

The wealth of information to be found in *The Linguistic Atlas* and similar studies, particularly those dealing with regional and social variations in pronunciation, can be used to augment the vocabulary and syntactic differences found in fiction. Such use serves to broaden the student's awareness that authors who make this kind of language difference a part of their work do so with great care and deliberation and that the differences are not merely peculiar or comic but represent acute sensitivity to language and a very real integrity on the part of the writer.

GRAMMATICALITY   All forms of creative and imaginative writing allow the writer certain liberties with English grammatical patterns. These departures, when they are made deliberately and with a firm grasp on the part of the writer that they do represent stretching, bending, or outright breaking of the grammatical systems of English, create an extra element of tension and impact. Working for this kind of effect often represents the creative writer's craft at its most difficult. When rules are broken by poets and authors of recognized worth, it is safe to say that such rule-breaking is done with deliberation and care and is not simply playful disregard of authority or, worse, carelessness. The best way to demonstrate this for students is to consider carefully which rules have been broken and how and then to note what effect the deviation produces. If the students are in good control of the standard grammatical patterns of English they can conduct this kind of investigation on their own—discovery method in its purest form!

LITERATURE IN TRANSLATION   Recognition of the fact that systems differ from one language to another can serve as the basis for serious consideration of the problems confronting translators of the great works of world literature originally written in a language other than English. Many students who maintain that they do not care for Homer or Dante or Chekhov base that opinion on a reading of faulty translations. School officials and teachers who make choices among translations are usually careful to evaluate the quality of the translations available. Students who make such choices for extra or outside reading assignments should be made aware of the critical nature of their choice.

They should know that something is always lost in translation and their best hope is to choose a translator who has kept such losses to a minimum.

The student need not be asked to take the teacher's word for the fact that translations vary from excellent to awful. Such differences are quite easily demonstrated by reading several translations of the same passage from a foreign literary work. Terribly inadequate versions to compare with the best of English translations are, unfortunately, very easy to find.

The systems of language are both the materials and the tools of the literary artist. The tremendously rich store of literature in the English language can be investigated, studied, understood, and appreciated in several ways. Studies based on aesthetic evaluation, philosophical contrasts, and interpretations of an author's intent are sometimes difficult to pin down; but differences in the manner in which various authors manipulate their materials and their tools can be discussed with a relatively high degree of precision if the student knows something of the systems and patterns of the English language.

17

LINGUISTICS AND THE TEACHING OF COMPOSITION

Linguistic scholars lay great stress on the primacy of speech, but much of what they have learned from their study of the systems and patterns of spoken English can be applied to the teaching of composition. If written language is a representation of speech sounds and the initial steps in the speech process involve ideation and the formulation of a language statement, then we are forced to conclude that the student who cannot think cannot write. But normal children do speak and often their imagination is limited only by the patience of their elders. Some children are more verbally aggressive than others, some have more vivid imaginations, and some are more fortunate in the environmental stimulation that has nurtured their innate language gift in their early, formative years. These variables make it unreasonable if not downright absurd to suppose that linguistics can produce a panacea for all the problems of the teacher of composition. These teachers know that all students cannot be taught to write equally well, but they also know that many of their students speak much more easily and effectively than they write. It seems only fair to assume that the study of the speech systems and patterns of English will produce some information that can be used to help students bring their writing skills to some reasonable approximation of their oral skills.

LANGUAGE SYSTEMS AND COMPOSITION

PHONOLOGY   Too often, in an attempt to help students negotiate the leap from spoken to written language, composition teachers suggest that they "just write it the way you would say it." The most important single fact about the sound system of English, as far as the teaching of composition is concerned, is that English speakers make many differences of meaning clear in ways that do not have written symbols. Some of the distinctions made by variations in stress, pitch and juncture can be indicated by punctuation, but most cannot. Students do not often recognize this fact until it is demonstrated for them.

One means of demonstrating the importance of stress in the communication of different meanings is to shift the emphasis around in a single simple sentence. For example:

SAM likes all the boys in our class.
Sam LIKES all the boys in our class.
Sam likes ALL the boys in our class.
Sam likes all the BOYS in our class.
Sam likes all the boys in OUR class.

Native speakers of English immediately recognize the differences that these shifts of stress signal. Students must be shown ways to make these distinctions clear by means of written language.

Some students who are told to "write it the way you would say it" attempt to commit intonations to paper by means of underlining stressed words or writing them in capital letters, and by making lavish use of exclamation points, dashes, series of dots, and parentheses. These methods are usually more distracting than they are helpful. Written language has its own conventions for establishing distinctions made by many of the stress patterns of speech. To return to the example sentences above, there are several specific meanings signalled by the capitalized words in each sentence. These meanings can be established in other ways.

Spoken: SAM likes all the boys in our class.
Written: Not everyone likes all the boys in our class, but Sam does.
Spoken: Sam LIKES all the boys in our class.
Written: Sam does like all the boys in our class.
Spoken: Sam likes ALL the boys in our class.
Written: There is not a single boy in our class that Sam dislikes.

Spoken: Sam likes all the BOYS in our class.
Written: Sam has his differences with some of the girls in
            our class, but he likes all the boys.
Spoken: Sam likes all the boys in OUR class.
Written: Sam likes all the boys in our class but he doesn't
            like some of those in other classes.

The written versions suggested here are only a few of the possible ways that written syntactic patterns can satisfactorily express the meanings lost with the intonation patterns of spoken English.

MORPHOLOGY   When words are taken apart so that the inflectional and derivational signals in English may be seen in isolation and recognized as units of meaning in themselves, these meanings can be explored and made clearer to student writers. The lapses in choosing the correct form of a noun, verb, adjective, or adverb for a given context that are so frequently noted in student papers is often the result of an inadequate knowledge of the inflectional and derivational forms of English and how they work. Many inflections in English are not distinct from others in sound or spelling. Some English nouns have *-s* endings that signal plurality, the possessive case, and the possessive plural. English verbs have the same ending for use with third person singular subjects; English regular verbs have both past and past participle forms ending in *-ed;* and a form ending in *-ing* may be either noun, verb or adjective. If the student is aware that these stumbling blocks lie in his path, he can guide his thinking and writing accordingly. Presenting the information about the gerund, or noun forms ending in *-ing* in one section of the grammar, the present participle verb forms in another and the adjectival use of these forms in still another is not enough to focus the attention of students on the real nature of the problem. The three separate activities of forms ending in *-ing* should be set side by side and clarified.

The study of derivational affixes should include adequate warning that the workings of these forms is not as regular as the workings of inflectional forms. Many highly imaginative but nonexistent words might never survive the first draft of a student paper if the writer were aware of the limited use allowed the derivational affixes in English.

SYNTACTIC PATTERNS AND TRANSFORMATION   The greatest contribution that linguistic research has to offer the teacher of composition is recognition of the tremendous burden carried by word order in the grammar of the English language.

Awkwardly constructed sentences, sentence fragments, and run-on sentences are all problems related to a lack of awareness among student writers that word order in English sentences is quite systematic and made up of reliably fixed patterns. While relationships holding between words, phrases and clauses in English are often signaled by function words, many of these relationships rest most heavily on the sequences in which the words appear in sentences.

Teaching any skill, whether it be art or music, carpentry or plumbing, baseball, or gardening, begins with teaching the names of tools and some of the ways that those tools can be used. Beginners are given simple tasks designed to build basic skills and are then assigned more and more challenging work. The learning of basic sentence patterns, writing sentences according to the patterns, learning to expand those sentences in simple ways, and progressing to more complex methods of expansion follows the procedure above in order to build composition skills.

Structural grammar provides useful devices for identifying the materials and tools of the writer's craft; sentence patterns or the phrase structure rules of generative grammar are effective means of defining the ways that the parts of the English language may be used in simple sentences.

Generative grammar makes several very helpful devices available to students and teachers of composition. The auxiliary rewrite rule gives the student a means of exploring the subtleties of meaning expressed by the various combinations of modals, auxiliary verbs, and verb forms possible in simple English sentences, and an easily used check on his own use of the combinations and forms.

Simple, single base transforms demonstrate most graphically the mobility of modifying words and phrases. For example, the teacher might begin with patterns including the simplest adverbs and adverbial prepositional phrases, and demonstrate which types of adverbs move and where. Simple lexical substitution for the patterns could be suggested by the teacher or provided by the students. The teacher might then progress to demonstration of the ways in which whole clauses operate—and move—as simple adverbs move.

A distinct advantage of describing the kernel sentences of English and the basic sentence types by means of symbolic formulas is that the nature of one of the more confusing problems of English verb forms is clearly specified. The fact that *be* and *have* may act as auxiliary verbs in some constructions and as full verbs in others causes difficulty for many student writers. The formulas clearly separate the positions and functions of the auxiliaries *be* and *have* from those of the full verbs *be* and *have*. A considerable number of sentence fragments result from the confusion among students as to the workings of these forms.

As more complex patterns are learned and particularly when students grasp the principles of transformation which allow them to turn simple sentences into modifying phrases and clauses, students begin to appreciate the flexibility and adaptability of the syntactic patterns of the English language. It often comes as a delightful surprise to some students that there is more than one correct way to combine their ideas into perfectly grammatical English sentences. If they have been taught several transformations they can be given sets of simple sentences and asked to combine them in a variety of ways. For example, several simple sentences such as

> The girl was talented.
> The girl played the music beautifully.
> The music was written by Chopin.

can be combined in several ways that are equally correct grammatically. Each possibility places greater importance on one or the other of the ideas involved. Choices among the possibilities are the writer's. The final choice is—or should be—that which best expresses the precise meaning the writer wishes to communicate.

Often two or more choices stress the same ideas. For example:

> The talented girl played the Chopin music beautifully.
> The girl, who was talented, played the music by Chopin beautifully.

A choice between them is a stylistic one. Students of composition often develop a style of their own intuitively. Those who have great difficulty in doing so—and they are in the majority—can be shown the alternatives open to them in sentence patterning and allowed to exercise choice among the possibilities. Teachers who correct an awkwardly worded sentence should be willing and able to demonstrate several possible ways of putting the sentence into grammatically acceptable form.

An awareness of some of the principles involved in organizing ideas for the greatest possible clarity in sentences should provide a sound basis for teaching the principles of paragraph and composition organization.

Finally, it is not unreasonable to suppose that exercises in sentence expansion and transformation will have the effect of stimulating the imagination and creativity of student writers. The search for alternatives in writing frequently triggers a new way of looking at the subject, another detail that might be included or even a whole new train of thought. At the very least, study of sentence patterns and transformation may make the student comment "Yes, I thought of that but I didn't know how to say it." less frequently heard by the teacher of composition.

SUGGESTED READING

ON THE NATURE OF LANGUAGE

Carroll, John B., ed. *Language, Thought and Reality: Selected Writings of Benjamin Lee Whorf.* Cambridge, Mass.: Technology Press, M. I. T., 1956.

Gleason, Henry A., Jr. *An Introduction to Descriptive Linguistics,* rev. ed. New York: Holt, Rinehart and Winston, Inc., 1961. Chap. 1.

Hall, Robert A., Jr. *Linguistics and Your Language.* New York: Doubleday and Company, Inc., 1950. (paperback)

Sapir, Edward. *Language: An Introduction to the Study of Speech.* New York: Harcourt, Brace & World, Inc., 1921.

ON THE HISTORY OF LANGUAGE STUDY

Dineen, Francis P. *An Introduction to General Linguistics.* New York: Holt, Rinehart and Winston, Inc., 1967.

Dykema, Karl W. "Where Our Grammar Came From," *College English,* April, 1961. Reprinted in *Readings in Applied English Linguistics,* second ed., Harold B. Allen, ed. New York: Appleton-Century-Crofts, 1964.

Gleason, Henry A., Jr. *Linguistics and English Grammar.* New York: Holt, Rinehart and Winston, Inc., 1965. Chaps. 2–3.

Robins, R. H. *A Short History of Linguistics.* Bloomington, Ind.: Indiana University Press, 1968.

ON THE HISTORY OF THE ENGLISH LANGUAGE

Baugh, Albert C. *A History of the English Language,* second ed. New York: Appleton-Century-Crofts, 1957.

Francis, W. Nelson. *The English Language: An Introduction.* New York: W. W. Norton & Company, Inc., 1965. Chap. 3.

Jespersen, Otto. *Growth and Structure of the English Language,* ninth ed. New York: Doubleday & Company, Inc., 1955. (paperback)

Robertson, Stuart. *The Development of Modern English,* second ed. Revised by Frederic G. Cassidy. Englewood Cliffs, N. J.: Prentice-Hall, Inc., 1954.

SCHOLARLY TRADITIONAL GRAMMARS

Curme, George O. *A Grammar of the English Language,* 2 vols. Boston: D. C. Heath and Company, 1931–1935.

Jespersen, Otto. *Essentials of English Grammar.* New York: Henry Holt and Company, Inc., 1933. Reprinted, University of Alabama Press, 1964.

Long, Ralph B. *The Sentence and Its Parts: A Grammar of Contemporary English.* Chicago: University of Chicago Press, 1961.

Poutsma, Hendrik. *A Grammar of Late Modern English,* second ed. Groningen, Netherlands: P. Noordhoff, N. V., 1914–1929.

Zandvoort, R. W. *A Handbook of English Grammar.* London: Longmans, Roberts and Green, 1957.

ON TRADITIONAL GRAMMAR IN THE SCHOOLS

Gleason, Henry A., Jr. *Linguistics and English Grammar.* New York: Holt, Rinehart and Winston, Inc., 1965. Chap. 1.

Harsh, Wayne. *Grammar Instruction Today.* Davis, Calif.: University of California, Davis, 1965. (pamphlet)

ON DESCRIPTIVE LINGUISTICS

Bloomfield, Leonard. *Language.* New York: Holt, Rinehart and Winston, Inc., 1933.

Gleason, H. A., Jr. *An Introduction to Descriptive Linguistics.* New York: Holt, Rinehart and Winston, Inc., 1961.

Hockett, Charles F. *A Course in Modern Linguistics.* New York: The Macmillan Company, 1958.

STRUCTURAL GRAMMARS

Francis, W. Nelson. *The Structure of American English.* New York: The Ronald Press Company, 1958.

Fries, Charles C. *The Structure of English.* New York: Harcourt, Brace and Company, Inc., 1952.

Hill, Archibald A. *An Introduction to Linguistic Structures.* New York: Harcourt, Brace and Company, Inc., 1958.

Roberts, Paul. *Patterns of English.* New York: Harper & Row, Publishers, 1956.

Sledd, James. *A Short Introduction to English Grammar.* Glenview, Ill.: Scott, Foresman and Company, 1959.

Stageberg, Norman C. *An Introductory English Grammar.* New York: Holt, Rinehart and Winston, Inc., 1965.

Trager, George L. and Henry Lee Smith, Jr. *An Outline of English Structure.* Studies in Linguistics, Occasional Papers, No. 3. Washington, D. C.: American Council of Learned Societies, 1957.

ON DIALECT GEOGRAPHY

Allen, Harold B. "The Linguistic Atlases: Our New Resource," *The English Journal,* April, 1956. Reprinted in *Readings in Applied English Linguistics,* second ed., Harold B. Allen, ed. New York: Appleton-Century-Crofts, 1964.

Atwood, E. Bagby. *A Survey of Verb Forms in the Eastern United States.* Ann Arbor, Mich.: University of Michigan Press, 1953.

Kurath, Hans. *A Word Geography of the Eastern United States.* Ann Arbor, Mich.: University of Michigan Press, 1949.

———— and Raven I. McDavid, Jr. *The Pronunciation of English in the Atlantic States.* Ann Arbor, Mich.: University of Michigan Press, 1961.

McDavid, Raven I., Jr. "American English Dialects" in *The Structure of American English* by W. Nelson Francis. New York: The Ronald Press Company, 1958.

ON SOCIAL DIALECTS

Labov, William. *The Social Stratification of English in New York City.* Washington, D. C.: Center for Applied Linguistics, 1966.

McDavid, Raven I., Jr. *American Social Dialects.* Champaign, Illinois: National Council of Teachers of English, 1965.

Shuy, Roger, ed. *Social Dialects and Language Learning.* Champaign, Illinois: National Council of Teachers of English, 1965.

ON USAGE

Bryant, Margaret M. *Current American Usage.* New York: Funk & Wagnalls Company, 1962.

Joos, Martin. *The Five Clocks.* Bloomington, Ind.: Indiana University Press, 1962.

Kenyon, John S. "Cultural Levels and Functional Varieties," *College English,* October, 1948. Reprinted in *Readings in Applied English Linguistics,* second ed., Harold B. Allen, ed. New York: Appleton-Century-Crofts, 1964.

ON TRANSFORMATIONAL-GENERATIVE THEORY

Bach, Emmon. *An Introduction to Transformational Grammars.* New York: Holt, Rinehart and Winston, Inc., 1964.

Chomsky, Noam. *Syntactic Structures.* New York: Gregory Lounz Book Company, 1957.

———— *Aspects of the Theory of Syntax.* Cambridge: M. I. T. Press, 1965.

Viertel, John. "Generative Grammars," *College Composition and Communication,* May, 1964.

TRANSFORMATIONAL-GENERATIVE GRAMMARS

Aurbach, Joseph, and Philip H. Cook, Robert B. Kaplan, Virginia Tufte. *Transformational Grammar: A Guide for Teachers.*

Washington, D. C.: English Language Services, Division of Educational Research Associates, Inc., 1967.

Goodman, Ralph. "Transformational Grammar" in *An Introductory English Grammar* by Norman C. Stageberg. New York: Holt, Rinehart and Winston, Inc., 1965.

Jacobs, Roderick A., and Peter S. Rosenbaum. *English Transformational Grammar.* Waltham, Mass.: Blaisdell Publishing Co., 1968.

Roberts, Paul. *English Syntax.* New York: Harcourt, Brace & World, Inc., 1964.

———— *Modern Grammar.* New York: Harcourt, Brace & World, Inc., 1968.

Thomas, Owen. *Transformational Grammar and the Teacher of English.* New York: Holt, Rinehart and Winston, Inc., 1967.

ON LINGUISTICS AND THE TEACHING OF LITERATURE AND COMPOSITION

Chatman, Seymour, and Samuel R. Levin, eds. *Essays on the Language of Literature.* Boston: Houghton Mifflin Company, 1967.

Christensen, Francis. *Notes Toward a New Rhetoric.* New York: Harper & Row, 1967.

Love, Glen A., and Michael Payne. *Contemporary Essays on Style.* Glenview, Ill.: Scott, Foresman and Company, 1969.

INDEX

Biblhog
197→

Str Analy of Syntax
98→ (spel diagrs)